The Venetians:
Merchant Princes

The Venetians:
Merchant Princes

THOMAS CALDECOT CHUBB

The Viking Press
New York

The woodcut panels on the title page are from
Mattia Pagan's *Procession of the Doge in St. Mark's
Square on Palm Sunday*, Museo Correr, Venice.

Chapter-head drawings by Laurel Toohey

To Russell and Lee,

and when they grow older,

to Rebecca, Tom III,

and Christopher

Contents

"The Fairest and Most Pleasant City of This Day and Age"

More than seven hundred years ago, a man with keen eyes and an observant spirit looked out of his window upon a scene that filled him with the same wonder and amazement with which Venice fills us even today. Then he took up his peacock-feather pen and carefully set down a description of the place in which he was.

"In the year of the Incarnation of our Lord 1267," he began, "I, Martino da Canale, did labor and endure until I had found out the ancient story of the Venetians, and whence they had come, and how they made Venice the fairest and noblest and most pleasant city of this day and age, and the most beautiful and the wealthiest in the world, for indeed merchandise gushes through it as does water in a fountain.

"It stands beside the sea," he continued, "and the salt water flows through it and around it. Indeed, this salt water is everywhere except in the houses and the streets. When the citizens are in the piazzas, they can return to their homes either by water or by land."

Venice buzzed with activity. "Those who do business here," Martino wrote, "come from all over the world and what they buy they can take back with them." And there was much to buy. "Provisions are abundant. There is bread and wine in plenty, and there are land fowl and waterfowl. There is fresh meat and salted meat and there are great fish from the rivers and the sea."

Martino described the inhabitants too. "Within the city there are numerous noblemen and noble youths, and they all deserve praise for their high conduct. There are also merchants, and bankers, and tradesmen who practice every kind of trade, and sailors of every sort. The latter man the ships that go to every part of the world and the great galleys that do hurt to the enemy. There are also fair matrons, and fair damsels, and fair young girls in great number, and every one of them is richly dressed."

One could almost say the city itself was richly dressed. At any rate, it seemed so to Martino. "St. Mark's," he said, "is the most beautiful piazza in the world. Toward the east is the most beautiful church in the world, the Church of My Lord, Messer St. Mark, and next to it is the Palace of the Doge. The latter is large in size, and marvelously beautiful. It is in that part of the piazza"—today we call it the piazzetta, or little piazza—"which runs toward the water. On the opposite side are the palaces of the citizens. These extend as far as the *campanile* (bell tower) of St. Mark. This bell tower is so tall that there is none like it anywhere. Next to it is a hospital (a charity hospital) which the doge's wife has had built to take care of the sick. Then come the palaces of the treasurers. These are called the procurators of St. Mark. Next to these are the palaces of the noblemen."

To be sure, there were still wooden shacks on parts of this mighty square, horses and even cattle grazed on it, and its present-day wide expanse was bisected by a *rio* (small canal). But when the doge (the chief magistrate of Venice), wearing his pearl-decked crown, moved through it in solemn procession, he had every reason to be proud.

This is what Martino wrote down, and since he wrote it in French and so must have been either a Frenchman or an Italian who had lived in France, he probably had traveled all the way from France to get there. If so, he would have crossed the snow-clad Alps, descended onto the Lombard plain, and then drifted down the Po River. The Po valley was the most fertile part of Italy, and although it had been devastated by centuries of war, his eyes must have gleamed at what he saw.

Mile after mile of fields of fertile grain with red poppies growing among the wheat. Herds of lowing cattle that fattened on green grass. Vines that were heavy with delicious grapes. (The wines of northern Italy were famous then and still are.) And then city after walled city that was like a jewel upon a necklace.

Milan was the biggest of them. It had been twice destroyed by a German emperor only a century before, but now, under its Visconti lords, it had risen from ashes and begun to flourish once again—so much so that sacks of surplus grain had to be stored in the cloisters of its many churches.

Nearby Pavia, once the capital of the Lombard kings, was almost as prosperous. It was still a capital—the summer capital of the dukes of Milan. The Italian poet Petrarch said he had never been in a place with such cooling breezes and refreshing showers. A century after Martino, he called the palace there "the most noble production of modern art."

These were only two of many—Piacenza, once upon a time Roman Placentia, and either the first or the second

Roman colony north of the Apennines; Ferrara with its own fierce rulers and angry, reddish walls; Mantua, where stilt-legged cranes waded in the three marshy lakes which surrounded it; Verona, the home—and at almost exactly this time—of Romeo and Juliet; Padua, called Padua the Learned because the second most important university in Italy was there. And more: Asti, Como, Cremona, Bergamo, Brescia, Vicenza.

Nowhere else in the Western world was there such an array of cities. Not even in Flanders (today Belgium). Certainly not in England or France.

But Martino had not seen the most dazzling city of all until he reached Venice. He still had not seen the glittering cluster of roofs and domes that seemed to rise, as if by enchantment, from a sea that was lavender and rose-colored and frail green as the morning mists wreathed it, and blue and crimson and gold in the noonday sun. When he did, he forgot the others.

But this old-time writer was not the only stranger to come to Venice and to paint a glowing picture of it. In 1494, the little hunchbacked French king, Charles VIII, set out to conquer Italy by simply marching through it, and at about that time he sent an ambassador to the canal city. He wanted to make sure that Venice would be on his side, or at least that she would not be against him. The man Charles sent was Philippe de Commines, and he was not only a skilled diplomat but one of France's great historians. He too set down his impressions.

He told of twenty-five young lords "finely and richly clad in robes of silk and scarlet" in a fleet of *piatte* (barges), each of which had a crimson awning and carpeted floor boards, and could carry forty persons. He described the Grand Canal. "It is the finest street in the world!" he said, noting that he had seen more than one four-hundred-ton galley moored in front of palaces whose façades were white marble, porphyry (deep-red marble), and serpentine (dull-green marble).

Philippe was taken to the Doge's Palace, "a fair and rich edifice crusted with gilt at least half an inch thick." The arsenal, he said, was the finest in the world and the best ordered for its kind of business. He marveled at the heaped-up silver and gold in the Treasury, which even the doge could not spend without the approval of his councilors, at the bejeweled crowns worn by the women on certain state occasions, and at the city's seventy or more beautiful churches and monasteries.

This was his conclusion: "Venice is the most triumphant city I have ever seen. It is the one that does the greatest honor to ambassadors and foreigners. It is the one where the service of God is the most solemnly observed. It may have faults. It does. But I firmly believe that the Almighty forever guides its destinies."

This was a Frenchman speaking. But an Italian praised Venice too.

His name was Pietro Aretino, and because this handsome black-bearded literary ruffian was already famed throughout all of Italy, Venice received him royally. He repaid her with lavish eulogies, saying that he would be content to stay there forever.

"When I die," he told a friend, "I would like to have God change me into a gondola or its canopy; or if that is too much, into an oar or a tholepin or a polishing rag; or into the scoop with which they bail it out; or, to name something more appropriate"—his enemies said he lived by sponging off people—"into a sponge; or even into one of those small copper coins with which they pay the ferrymen." Anything

—so long as he would not have to leave "carefree, liberal, and just Venice."

He gave some very good reasons for his feelings about the city. "I never look out of my window," he said, "that I do not see a thousand merchants in as many gondolas."

These were going to the nearby markets—to the booths of the butchers and the fishmongers on the right; to the German warehouse on the left; some, to the Rialto itself.

"There are grapes in the barges, game and pheasants in the shops, vegetables laid out on the pavements."

In fact, the canal itself was an emporium. Floating on it below his window would be twenty to twenty-five sailboats, laden with melons, and drawn together to form a sort of island.

"To them," wrote Aretino, "the crowd hurries to count, to sniff, and to weigh, so as to find out whether they are in good condition or not. All is hurly-burly."

Even the Venetian housewives as they went about their daily business were resplendent—they were not the plain Janes of other less fortunate places.

"They gleam in silk and gold and jewels. I will not speak of this, however. I do not want to seem to boast. But I will say that I nearly split my sides laughing at the whistles, the catcalls, and the jeers with which the boatmen followed those who were rowed by servants who did not wear scarlet hose."

Aretino and a friend almost split their sides laughing too when a boatload of Germans came staggering out of a tavern, capsized their vessel, and were hurled into the canal.

"Orange trees gild the base of the Palace of the Chamberlains"—Aretino could see it from his balcony—"and lights twinkle the whole night long in those places were they sell food and wine. Music tinkles through the dusk. Nor must I forget [to mention] the great foreign lords who continually pass me in the streets. Nor the Bucentaur (the official ducal barge) plying hither and yon. Nor the regattas. Nor the festivals. There is no end of them."

All this and a great deal more—and they were mostly things that only money could buy. Only money, but there was plenty of it. "You should visit Venice," Aretino told a second friend, "if you want other cities to seem like poorhouses!"

Even a king could be impressed by Venice—and a pope too.

The king was Henry III of France, who visited the city in 1574 on his way from Poland to Paris to claim the throne of France.

He landed at Murano—the nearby island of the glass blowers—and there he was met by sixty senators who presented him with a brilliantly painted gondola that had a canopy of cloth of gold. The next day the doge himself came to greet Henry in the Bucentaur and, with its four hundred oars beating the water, took him to the Lido, where he was shown a special arch of triumph made in his honor and decorated with paintings by a great artist. Then he was conducted back to Venice and to the palace, where he was to be lodged.

The following days were a long sequence of celebrations and shows. There were regattas, fireworks, a sham battle with padded clubs during which many contestants were thrown into the canal, a banquet which three hundred persons attended, and a gala ball. To impress the young king even more, the building of a great galley was begun and finished during the short time he was in Venice. Some say that its keel was laid when he sat down at the banquet and it was launched before he arose.

But it was a midnight supper that pleased Henry most of all. As he sat down, he started to pick up his napkin. It crumbled in his hand, for it was made of sugar, as were all the many statues that adorned the royal table. Yet so skillfully had it been fashioned that it seemed to be real folds of real linen.

Henry clapped his hands in delight. "Oh, if only my mother could have been here to see this!" he cried.

His mother was the tradesman's daughter—that is what the French nobles snobbishly called her because her great-grandfather had been a banker—Catherine de' Medici!

The pope visited Venice many centuries earlier. He was Pope Alexander III, who reigned from 1159 to 1181.

He came in 1176, but his coming was not marked by the pomp and circumstance which might be expected when the head of the Church visited an important city. Instead, he came as an unknown fugitive, for Emperor Frederick Barbarossa (the Frederick Redbeard who had twice destroyed Milan) refused to recognize him, and had one antipope and then another named in his place. Alexander had been obliged to flee from Rome, and disguised as a poor pilgrim, cold and hungry, he wandered through Italy until, in Venice, he found refuge in a monastery, where he worked as a scullion.

There he washed cauldrons and scoured pots for six months before a French monk recognized him and informed his superiors. Every bell in Venice tolled at the news. Then a mighty procession was formed, and Alexander was borne in triumph to the palace of the patriarch. Here, with the doge standing beside him, he ordered Frederick to end his defiance of the Church and to recognize him as pope. After all, he had been chosen by a majority of the cardinals!

At first the emperor refused, but when a Venetian fleet of thirty galleys defeated an imperial fleet of sixty, Frederick had to change his mind. Moreover, in token of his submission, he was forced to strip himself of his crown and royal garments and lie down upon the ground before Alexander, who then put his foot upon the Redbeard's neck.

Alexander was exultant. "There is no city like Venice!" he cried.

And to make sure that everybody knew he meant this, he issued a papal proclamation saying that from thenceforward Venice should be the sovereign and the lord husband of the sea. Alexander meant the Adriatic Sea, but the Venetians took it to mean all oceans, and from then on, every year on Ascension Day, they performed a solemn ceremony.

On that day, the doge sailed out of the Porto di Lido in the same enormous golden barge—*Bucintauro*, the Italian name for the Bucentaur, comes from *bucio d'oro* (barge of gold)—with which the Venetians greeted Henry III. A procession of other barges carrying officials followed him, and behind them came everything that would float, from great galleys to little skiffs.

Once they had reached the high sea, the flotilla halted. The bishop then took out a ring. He blessed it and handed it to the doge, who took it and flung it into the water.

"*Desponsamus te, mare,*" he intoned solemnly, "*in signum veri perpetuique domini.* O Sea, we here do wed thee in our true and everlasting rule over thee."

Then the flotilla returned, every craft in it festooned with laurel and flowers. The night that followed would be a night of singing and celebration.

It would be difficult to say how much this annual ceremony cost; it must have been a fortune. But Venice could afford it. Except for the fabled cities of Cathay (China) and India, and possibly Constantinople and Alexandria, she was the richest city in the world.

How did this come to pass?

Venice—and her wealth and glory—did not just happen. She was created slowly and deliberately by men who knew what they wanted. And she rose to her great heights from the most modest beginnings.

The Marsh Gauls Become the Venetians

At one time, and very long ago, the land that was later called Venetia was uninhabited. But so, too, was almost every land in the world before *Homo sapiens* (man, the knowing one—that is our name for ourselves) began his step-by-step emigration from Africa or wherever he began.

Indeed, at one time, it was not even the same land. If you look at a map of Europe, you will see Italy thrusting southward like a foot kicking a football (Sicily), and between Italy on one side and the mountains of Albania and Dalmatia on the other side is the long, narrow body of water which today we call the Adriatic Sea. But this body of water had not always been a sea. On the middle of the calf of our imaginary leg is the city of Ancona, and during the last glacial period (about twenty thousand years ago) the water receded as far as this or even farther. One could have walked dry-shod across what is now salt water. At other times, the sea advanced to the very foothills of the Alps or even into some of the Alpine valleys.

But finally (between 8000 and 10,000 B.C.), the earth—

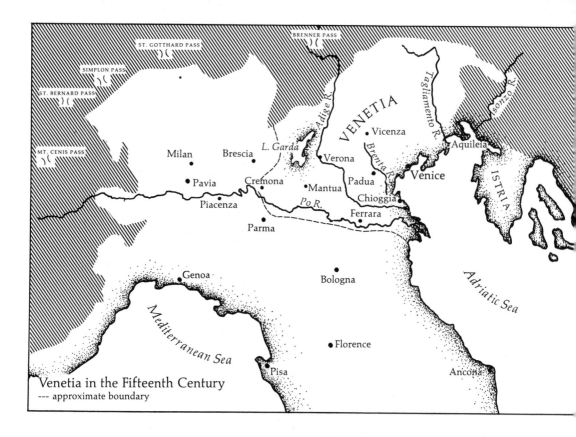

Venetia in the Fifteenth Century
--- approximate boundary

and its climate—settled down, and Venetia (northeast Italy between the Po and Isonzo rivers and the Alps) took its present, or almost its present, form. In 21 A.D. the Greek geographer Strabo described it as follows.

"The whole country is full of rivers, especially in the northwest, and this area also experiences tides like those of the ocean. It is the only part of the Mediterranean to do so. In consequence, there are many lagoons. In these, the inhabitants have dug canals and built dikes as they do in the land of Egypt. In that way, some of the regions are drained and cultivated but other parts of it are navigable."

These lagoons were divided, as they are today, into *le lagune vive* (the live lagoons), which together formed a great salt lake, with here and there little hummocks; and *le lagune morte* (the dead lagoons), a malarial salt marsh.

Both were protected from the sea by a long series of low, narrow sand-bar islands which the Venetians called *lidi*. (The famous Lido, now an internationally renowned bathing resort with crowded beaches and *de luxe* hotels, is merely the largest and most important of these *lidi*.)

Behind them, to the west, was the mainland, with a *pineta* (fragrant pine forest) which stretched along its shore for a good hundred miles, and behind this was the plain of northern Italy, watered by the Po, the Brenta, the Adige, and other rivers. It was the widest and most fertile plain in southern Europe, and still is.

Human beings first came to this plain—and to the *pineta* too—after the last ice of the glaciers had retreated into the Alps. Even at that—and no one knows why—they did not come as soon as they did to other places in Europe. There were no men of the Old Stone Age in Venetia. But with the New Stone Age (scientists call it the Neolithic Age) it was something else again. Skin-clad hunters crossed the Alps to track down the chamois, wild goat, brown bear (even though they worshiped the bear), and wild boar, and to trap the marmot. But those who reached the plain, in time became farmers. They began to grow grain, cultivate grapes and fruit, and keep herds of sheep, hogs, and cattle. Their hunting dogs became sheep dogs. These New Stone Age men left many traces behind them. In this part of Italy one can find carefully chipped arrowheads, almond-shaped spear points, and sturdy hide scrapers, much like those made by the American Indians.

Around 3000 or 4000 B.C. the New Stone Age men were superseded by the Bronze Age men. There were many tribes of them. They too left beautifully wrought artifacts—hatchets, daggers, swords, and shields. But although traces of their blood, and as a matter of fact the blood of the

New Stone Age men too, may still flow in Venetian veins, only one group of these Bronze Age men made any real contribution to the Venice we know. These were the lake dwellers, who are sometimes also called the *terramare*, or land-sea, people. On Lake Garda and in other places, the lake dwellers built their villages over the water, and traveled to and from them in boats. One of these villages stood on ten thousand piles sunk into water six feet deep. It covered an acre and a half. Almost certainly it was from the *terramare* people that the Venetians learned that they could build homes, and even a city, where there wasn't any land.

But if these Bronze Age men—and the New Stone Age men—were not the true ancestors of the Venetians, there arrived in the area, around 1000 B.C., another people who really were. These were also the ones who gave the Venetians their name. They called themselves the Heneti, a name the Romans later changed to "Veneti." Students are still arguing about who they were and where they came from.

For Strabo, there were just two choices. "Some say," he tells us, "that they were a colony of those Celts of the same name who dwell by the ocean." These were the Veneti of southern Brittany, whose skill as sailors and whose ships with leather sails made such an impression on Julius Caesar when he finally conquered them.

"But others insist," Strabo continues, "that they are descendants of the Veneti of Paphlagonia (in Asia Minor) who came here after the fall of Troy."

We now know that the second choice is probably the right one. The Heneti almost certainly came from Asia Minor.

But in the olden days, most people believed in the first theory—that the Heneti came from Gaul—and so they became known as the Marsh Gauls. It was just about as good a name as any. In the beginning, they were not Gauls or even Celtic, but as time passed they began to live like Gauls and even to intermarry with them, and at a much later time some of them became dwellers in the marsh.

These newcomers took over the plain and the fertile valleys from the Bronze Age men who were there before them, and they too became farmers and herders. The Henetic horses were famous! But the Marsh Gauls became city dwellers—or at least town dwellers—too. Nor were their cities and towns merely haphazard collections of hovels. The houses were rectangular and well planned, and though they had humble thatched roofs, the walls were solid stone. There were city walls too; dry stone, but strong enough to withstand any assault by neighboring tribes. They were so well placed geographically that at least one of them, the little town of Este, is still a city today.

It might still be a Henetic city, except for one thing. Far to the south of Italy, near the old cones of a cluster of extinct volcanoes, two other Iron Age tribes, the Latins and the Sabines, founded a little group of small villages by the River Tiber, and around 753 B.C. these fused into one larger village, which became all-conquering Rome. Step by step, Rome took over almost all of Italy, and finally, in 232 B.C., the tough Roman legions marched into Heneti land. Their excuse was that they wanted to protect the Heneti from the Gauls (the *Marsh* Gauls from the *true* Gauls), but actually they wanted to protect the coastal highway to Illyria (modern Yugoslavia). They needed this to move their troops to the Balkans and to Asia Minor.

Obviously the Heneti could not hold them off, and soon the Romans took over this part of Italy too and renamed it Venetia. As with all the lands they conquered, they im-

mediately Romanized it. City after city was built in the
Roman style. Aquileia. Concordia. Altinum. Opitergium.
Padua. Verona. Each one had baths, temples, theaters,
aqueducts, and splendid houses. Roads were constructed
which penetrated into the most inaccessible places. To be
sure, the rude and rough-garbed natives were allowed to
remain, and most of them did. But they were forced to
adopt Roman ways. A Roman goddess took the place of
Reitiia, the time-honored Henetic goddess of health and
childbirth, with her long robes and her keys to the world
below. The Paleo-Venetian (Old Venetian) language gave
way to Latin. The squiggly, scratchy old Venetian alphabet
—some of the letters look like symbols on a weather map—
was replaced by the one that is used today.

It was at this time, or at any rate not very much later, that
some of the Heneti began drifting into the lagoon. There
they became fishermen, snarers of the web-footed marsh
and shore birds, saltmakers, and even gardeners.

Cassiodorus, a famous Roman author, describes how
they lived. He wrote several centuries later, but the picture
he painted was true from the very beginning.

"Although occasionally there is a wooden house," he
said, "for the most part [their] houses are made of mud and
wattle, and [these] are like the nests of sea birds, for sometimes they can be seen upon the land and sometimes on the
water. They are protected from the ocean waves. This means
[they] can navigate in any kind of weather. [Their] boats
have sails but [they] do not need the winds, nor do [they]
even need oars, for when the channel is too narrow to use
either, [the] people draw them"—by means of two lines
attached to a leather harness which was strapped to their
backs—"as they move along the embankment at a slow
walk. At that time, it almost seems as if [the boats] were

gliding across the grass, for these embankments are so high that you cannot see their hulls."

As they were later on in Venice, the Heneti dwellings were built on larch piles, and in front of each one of them was a small skiff. This was the ancestor of the gondola. It was secured to a *palo* (mooring pole), just as the owner's horse would have been tethered to a hitching post had he lived on the mainland. It had to be, for the Marsh Gaul, both before and after he became a Venetian, needed it for his fowling and fishing; or to take him to the nearby salt pans to turn the cylinders there—these cylinders, used for making salt, were as important to him as plows and pruning hooks were to farmers ashore; or to transport the fruits of his toil to the occasional Roman villa which could be found in the lagoons even in those ancient days.

All shared a rough-and-ready equality, Cassiodorus said. "Among the lagoons, the poor man and the rich man live in the same way. They have the same food and the same kind of dwelling places. Nor do they strive for gold as do the men who live in the cities. Their competition, when there is any, is for salt." This, and not minted coins, served them for money.

Roman rule did not last forever, however, and neither did the peace and tranquility it brought.

The descendants of the Tiber-valley farmers and shepherds had marched and conquered until they were masters not only of their own peninsula but of a good part of the whole known world. Their power extended from the borders of Scotland and Germany in one direction to Egypt, Mesopotamia, and southern Russia in the other. But then they had to move backward again as the people of the forests, steppes, and even deserts which they had once conquered began to think about conquering them.

Why not, these people began to ask themselves, storm into the lands held by the Romans and into the Roman cities? The Romans can no longer defend themselves. They have grown weak and soft. Why not seize all their wealth and treasure, and their wide fertile acres? This they soon commenced to do.

Starting as far back as 332, tribe after tribe—yellow-haired Goths and slit-eyed Huns and many others—came marching, riding, and raiding into the Roman Empire. And since Italy was the most famous and probably the wealthiest of all Roman provinces, sooner or later most of them invaded Italy.

Venetia and the Henetic-Roman cities stood in their way. Because peace had lasted so long, many of these cities had no walls. The walls of those that did were inadequate or had fallen into ruin. What could the inhabitants do? They had only two alternatives: fight and be killed or carried off as slaves—or flee. A few fought, but the majority fled. The Romanized Heneti fled to their cousins deep in the lagoons.

Martino da Canale is very specific about when and how this happened. "There was a pagan," he says, "called Attila (Attila the Hun), and this Attila came into Italy with five hundred men. And the first city he came to (Aquileia) he took and destroyed. The noblemen of the city and their ladies fled toward the sea at his approach, and they took with them all their gold and silver. There they found certain small islets, and on them built many beautiful cities. And this took place in the year of our Lord 421."

Not everybody agrees with him, however. In fact, most historians think that the real flight to the lagoons came almost a century and a half later. They say that the people of Aquileia may have fled from Attila, but that they came back, and that a mass flight, not merely from Aquileia but from all the mainland cities, did not begin until the Lombards arrived in 558.

There is an old Venetian legend which seems to support this version of the story. "When the Lombards came," it relates, "they came to the city of Altinum (now Altino, on the mainland northeast of Venice), and as they approached, the inhabitants could see the birds of the place rise from crannies in the walls and from the roofs and fly away. They bore their young in their beaks and the people of Altinum decided to follow them. One third went toward Istria (on the other side of the Adriatic), and another third to Ravenna, but the last third hesitated. As they were hesitating the bishop of Altinum heard a voice. 'Mount ye to the top of the tower,' it said, 'and look ye on the stars.' He obeyed and he could see the islands of the lagoons spread out before him. They seemed like stars to him."

It was a message from above, he knew. He descended as swiftly as he could, and faced those citizens who still waited. "Follow me!" he said. "Follow me! God has instructed us."

To the lagoon he led them, and then into boats, which took them to the nearest of the islands. There they founded Torcello, naming it—*torricella* means "little tower"—after the tower in Altinum. Except for Grado, which had been founded by refugees fleeing from Attila, it was the oldest of the little Venices—that is what they are called today—that were soon scattered all about the area.

For as the Romans and the Romanized Heneti sought safety in the swamps and marshes, they began to establish a dozen or so little towns.

Caorle was on a long sandy beach near the delta of the Tagliamento River. Equileum—now Iesolo—was on the same strand. Heracliana, the last of these little Venices to be founded, and for this reason called "the *new* city of

Heracliana," was not far distant. To the north, near Torcello, was Mazzorbo; although its name comes from the Latin *major urbs* (larger city), it is now little more than vineyards and vegetable gardens. And there were others. Rivo Alto (now Rialto). Malamocco on the Adriatic shore. Cluges Minor—modern Sottomarina. Cluges Major, which very soon became Chioggia.

In the beginning, these towns had little if any connection with one another, and some of them were small indeed. Malamocco, for example, was hardly more than a collection of fisherman's huts and hovels, and many of the others were not much bigger. But gradually they drew together and formed a loosely-bound league or alliance. This would one day become the Republic of Venice. In those early days, no one of them really dominated the others. Grado was the seat of the patriarch, and hence the religious capital. Its ancient cathedral still stands. Torcello—most visitors are drawn to it today only because of its two splendid Byzantine churches, in one of which is a wonderful tall deep-blue Madonna in mosaic—was the commercial center. Heracliana and Equileum took turns at being the political capital until finally, and because these two fought each other so bitterly, Malamocco became the seat of government.

But it was not until two hundred and fifty years after Torcello had been founded—when once again the marsh dwellers were threatened by invaders from the north, this time the Franks, a Germanic people who had settled in France and become French—that the city which gave its name and rule to all the other lagoon cities came into being. This was the city which we know as Venice, and it was built on the site where it still stands today.

For as these invaders marched through the mainland toward the shore, the inhabitants of the lagoons realized that Malamocco and even Heracliana or Equileum were too exposed to be easily defended. Deep in the lagoons, however, was a place that could be. "Rivo Alto" means deep stream, and that probably means that a navigable channel led to the island of that name. But it was a channel that twisted and meandered so that only people who knew it could use it. And near Rivo Alto were three other islands: Spinalunga (long backbone—today it is the Giudecca), Dorsodoro (hard back), and Olivolo. Joined together, they could make a stronghold that was both inaccessible and easy to supply.

Joined they were, and Venice, as the new city was shortly called, became the temporary capital. Soon the temporary capital became the permanent one, and before long it was the commercial center and the religious center too. All the other Venices either gradually died or faded into sleepy little settlements. But this Venice endured.

The City Reaches Out and Grows Great

Venice endured to become one of the world's most glorious cities, and to become the capital of a far-flung empire. But it did not do so without difficulties and a never-ending struggle.

Until the barbarian invasions, and even after the first of them, Venetia was part of the old Roman Empire—the old *Western* Roman Empire as in its latter days it was increasingly called. But when Rome finally fell in 476, this part of Italy transferred its allegiance to Byzantium (Constantinople) and became part of the Eastern Roman Empire, which was now the only Roman empire. In theory at least, this land of rude fishermen and half-savage bird snarers (that is what the haughty Byzantines called its inhabitants) became a Byzantine province and not even a self-governing one. And when, in 697, the men of the lagoons were finally allowed to elect their own head of state, he still acknowledged the Byzantine emperor as his overlord and dutifully told him he was proud to assume such Byzantine titles as *hypatos, protospatharius*, and patrician.

This state of affairs continued until 800. Then the former Western Roman Empire was revived, and the pope crowned the Frankish king, Charlemagne, as its first emperor. To be sure, he was only crowned Western Roman emperor, but that was enough for him. Forthwith he laid claim to every city that the old Western Roman Empire had ever ruled. That, of course, included Venetia. "It is mine!" the tall blond-bearded ruler cried. "Venetia and its lagoons and the people in them are mine!" And he ordered his scribes to scratch out a decree annexing it.

This accomplished nothing, for the Byzantine emperor at the time—she would not allow herself to be called empress—was a tough, fearless old woman, Irene, and she merely laughed. Let Charlemagne come and take them, she suggested. Who was he anyway but an ignorant barbarian who could neither read nor write and who had insulted her by offering to marry her.

But Irene did not rule forever, or even for long. In 802 she was overthrown by one of her generals, a man named Nicephorus, who had himself proclaimed emperor in her stead. Then it was another matter, for civil war raged through the land, and the new emperor did not want a foreign war as well. He sent word to Charlemagne that Venetia was his, and he didn't even ask the Venetians what they thought about this. Why should he? They were his subjects and his slaves.

Fortunately for the Venetians, however, their new lord was too busy to claim the domain which had been handed over to him—at any rate, for a while—and this gave them time to prepare. One of their preparations was to move their capital to where it stands today.

Actually, they had four years to prepare, for Nicephorus formally handed over Venetia and the lagoon towns, includ-

Milan

VENETIA

Venice

Genoa

Florence

Pisa

Zara

ITALY

DALMATIA

CORSICA

Adriatic Sea

Rome

Ragusa

SARDINIA

Naples

Amalfi

SICILY

Tunis

M
e
d
i
t

Republic of Venice and Territories
in the Sixteenth Century

Sea of Azov

Black Sea

OTTOMAN

Constantinople•

EMPIRE

Aegean Sea

RHODES

CYPRUS

CRETE

Beirut•
•Damascus

nean Sea

Alexandria•

•Cairo

Nile R.

EGYPT

ing Rivo Alto, in 806, and the Franks did not move until 810.

Then they went into action rapidly. Almost without warning, Frankish armies marched on Heracliana and Cluges Major—they took them both—and a Frankish fleet anchored off Malamocco. It was commanded by Charlemagne's son Pepin, who called on the Malamoccans to surrender.

There was no answer. And for a good reason. Malamocco was deserted except for one wizened old woman who paced up and down the beach and seemed to be seething with fury.

"They have deserted me," she told the Franks in explanation, "and gone to Rivo Alto. But I will be revenged, for I know the way to their secret hiding place and will lead you to it."

"Where is it?" the Franks asked.

"Deep in the lagoon."

They followed her along the shore until they came to a devious channel marked by stakes. This led to a wooden causeway.

"That will take you to them!"

Whether she was tricking them or was simply ignorant, nobody will ever know, but no sooner was the weight of the heavily armored Franks and their horses upon the frail structure than it collapsed. All of them were hurled into the water. Many of them drowned.

But even that did not discourage Pepin. With a few followers, he got into a boat and was pushed or rowed until he came to the palisaded Venetian stronghold. There he confronted the Venetians and their doge.

"Yield to me!" he commanded. "You are my subjects! My father is your master!"

"We have only one master—the emperor! The *Roman* emperor!" By Roman emperor, they meant the Byzantine emperor.

Pepin tried to parley with them, but they replied with shouts of defiance and a shower of missiles. Fortunately, he was out of range and they could not harm him. But he could not harm them either. His fleet was far off and could not be brought nearer. So he ordered his boatmen to take him back to Malamocco. There he boarded his flagship again and disconsolately sailed away.

That was the end of the Frankish attempt to take over, for Charlemagne, having heard his son's report, bowed to the inevitable and signed a new treaty in which he acknowledged that the allegiance of the Venetians belonged to the Byzantine emperor and not to himself. He never tried to conquer them again. To be sure, other Roman emperors of the West did. Otto II was one of them, and Frederick Barbarossa was another. But none of them succeeded. From now on Venice turned its eyes to the East.

From now on, too, Venice became increasingly its own master. It is true that the city did not formally sever its ties with its Byzantine overlords for another two hundred and sixty years, but long before that it paid lip service only to them, and for all practical purposes, managed its own affairs.

It was able to do this for two reasons.

First, Byzantium was too far away to exert any real control over Venice. By land, the road from Venice to Byzantium ran for a thousand miles through the rugged and mountainous Balkans, and here the land was infested with Slav and Hungarian marauders. If, on the other hand, one went by sea, it was necessary to round southern Greece, and then sail up the long and often stormy Ionian and Adriatic seas.

And second, the Byzantines needed help from Venice more than Venice needed help from them, for they were defending a large, widely extended empire which was under attack from every direction, by sea as well as by land.

Incidentally, Venice gave this help freely. It was greatly to her advantage to do so and the Venetians never lost a chance of doing something that would benefit them.

"Their character," says a man who knew them well, "was a mixture of selfishness and patriotism. In their make up, they combined unscrupulousness with self-denial, and stubborn self-will with the subordination of private self-interest to the well-being and glory of the state."

The Venetians lent their aid to Byzantium from the very earliest of days. In 552, for example, when the great Justinian was emperor and the Byzantines really did rule in Italy, the tough boatmen of the lagoons sent a flotilla of barges to his general, Narses, and moved the Byzantine army across the Adige River so that they could continue their southward march to attack and conquer the Goths.

At that time, the Venetians probably *had* to help the Byzantines, but at that time, too, the Byzantines probably learned how good they were at it.

At least from time to time, and when it suited them, they were still helping the Byzantines in the fifteenth century, when the Byzantine Empire, now near its end, was making a last stand against the Turk.

Nor did they help them only in time of war. In times of peace the Venetians carried Byzantine cargoes into places where the Byzantines could not or would not go—western Europe, for example—and they acted as Byzantine emissaries there too. In the end, they carried Byzantine cargoes everywhere, for the Byzantines gradually traded in their own vessels less and less.

But the Venetians could not have aided the Byzantines— and themselves—if they had not made themselves strong and feared, and this took them a little time to do, for even after Pepin had been forced to withdraw, they still had many enemies to fight.

Chief among these were the Arab corsairs and Dalmatian pirates, who raided the shoreline and attacked Venetian shipping. The Arabs caused them the least difficulty, for most Arab bases were no nearer than Sicily or North Africa. And although Arab vessels defeated a Venetian fleet off Ancona in 829—this is the first time Venetian naval vessels are mentioned in an official document—the Venetians could usually drive them off. But the Dalmatian pirates had many fine harbors and only the narrow Adriatic to cross. They did this frequently, burning and plundering. In 845—some historians say in 945—they even dared sail up to Venice itself.

This was when they almost captured the Venetian brides, a story which was long told in Venice. From the very earliest days, all Venetian weddings took place on February 1. The brides-to-be assembled at the Church of San Pietro di Castello on the island of Olivolo in the eastern part of the city. All carried their wedding portions in handsome painted caskets, and the bridegrooms awaited them at the church door. With the doge himself in attendance, the bishop first blessed the young couples and then married them. Gay festivals followed.

But one day the celebrations were suddenly interrupted. Pirates from the Narenta River in Dalmatia had learned of what was about to happen, and decided it was too good an opportunity to be lost. During the late hours of the night before the ceremony, they approached Venice in their ships and hid in the tall rushes which grew nearby. Then, at the height of the merrymaking, they made off with the struggling brides and their treasures.

They were not allowed to keep their booty long. Once the

bridegrooms had recovered from their shock, they raced to their boats and, followed by every able-bodied Venetian and led by the doge himself, pursued the raiders to Caorle. At Caorle—which from then on was known as the Porto delle Damigelle, or Young Ladies' Port—there was a bloody battle, and the pirates were defeated.

But even though the Venetians were able to rescue the brides, they still feared the marauders from the sea, and to protect their ships and shipping, they continued to pay tribute to them. Every year ambassadors from Venice went to the pirate strongholds bearing heavy sacks of gold.

Until the year 1000, that is. Then a strong doge, Pietro Orseolo II, sat upon the ducal throne. Instead of sending tribute, he assembled a fleet, and one balmy Ascension Day, sailed with it toward Istria. There he found a pirate fleet and routed it. Then he moved down the Dalmatian coast, attacking city after city that had been friendly to the pirates. One after another, they fell into his hands. They became Venetian cities, and they look like Venetian cities even today, although Slavs later moved into them and their population is now Slavic.

Pietro Orseolo then came home in triumph and proclaimed himself Duke of Dalmatia as well as Doge of Venice. The doges never gave up this title.

A little later the Venetians set up bases in Epirus (today southern Albania and northern Greece) and established friendly relations with the Italian cities on the other side of the Straits of Otranto, the narrow body of water that separates the heel of Italy from present-day Albania.

That was only the beginning, however, for the Narenta pirates were followed by Croat pirates and then by the Hungarians. After that, around 1080, a new enemy appeared. The Normans—the same one-time Vikings who had conquered England sixteen years before under William the Conqueror—sailed into the Mediterranean and landed in Sicily and southern Italy. Soon they were the masters of both. One of them, Robert Guiscard (Robert the Crafty), thought that an even greater prize could be gained. He would land in the Balkans, march to Constantinople, and make himself Byzantine emperor. Had it not been for the Venetians, he might have done just this. But they destroyed his fleet near Durazzo, and Alexius Comnenus stayed on his throne.

In gratitude, the emperor heaped every kind of privilege on the men from the lagoons, and particularly the right to do business throughout his empire under the most favorable terms possible. In consequence, Venetian trading posts were set up far and wide. In the Peloponnesus (southern Greece); in the Greek islands; at Salonika in Greece itself; at Candia (on Crete) and Cyprus; even on the shores of the Tana (Don) River, which flowed into the distant Sea of Azov. The Venetians were also given a quarter of their own in Constantinople. It had the best part of the city's water front, its own quays, shops, and houses, three or four churches, and even a bakery. It was a Venice away from home.

During the Crusades, Venice's position became even stronger. Venice, Pisa, and Genoa were the only cities in Europe with fleets large enough to transport those who wished to go to the Holy Land by sea. Venice took the lead in this enterprise, and she drove a hard bargain. The knights of western Europe, crying "God wills it!" and wearing the cross on their tunics and shields, might dream romantically of couching their lances against the turbaned Infidel and rescuing the Holy Sepulcher, but to the Venetians it was strictly business. They would get the Crusaders to their destination, and more important, they would keep them supplied with food and other provisions. But they would ask for and insist on receiving their pound of flesh.

Even so, they always lived up to every clause in the agreements they signed, and sometimes even went beyond the letter to the spirit. Between 1114 and 1124, for example, they joined the Crusaders in besieging Tyre, and when the operations took longer than expected, one of the latter turned to the Venetian admiral.

"We are here and must stay," he said. "But you have ships and you can sail away and leave us."

The admiral turned to one of his lieutenants. "Beach our vessels," he commanded. These were dragged onto the shore, and the admiral had a plank removed from below the water line of every one of them.

"Now we have to stay too," he told the Crusaders.

And until the victory was won and the city taken, the Venetians remained.

Thus Venice aided the Crusaders for a profit just as she had aided Byzantium with an eye to the rewards. But even this was not enough for the strong and aggressive state which Venice had now become. She wanted something much more solid and definite. She wanted to own in her own right and not merely be granted her advantages as a privilege. Furthermore, this was only practical. The person who gave you favors could take them away from you. But what you had and held as your own, you could keep.

It soon became plain that the Venetians were correct in thinking this. Alexius, as we have seen, needed their services and was happy to pay for them. But with his successors, it was another matter. Complaining that the Venetians were "arrogant," that "they did not even try to conceal their business sharpness," and "that they issued orders to us as if we were their slaves," these men began to harass them in every way. They imposed taxes on the Venetians, forced them to serve in the Byzantine army, and what was worse, encouraged the Pisans and the Genoese to send fleets into Byzantine waters and to compete where the Venetians thought they had been promised a monopoly.

Finally, on March 7, 1171, Emperor Manuel Comnenus struck a blow that could not be forgiven. He imprisoned every Venetian in his empire; seized every Venetian ship in Byzantine waters; and laid his hands on every bit of Venetian property he could. Eleven years later, his successor, Andronicus, did something even worse. He ordered the massacre of every Latin in his realm. Most of them were Venetians.

It was at that moment that Venice realized she must strike back. She and the Byzantines could no longer coexist peacefully in the same narrow Mediterranean world. One of them must go. Venice came to a decision. She decided that she must destroy the Byzantine Empire, and replace it with a Venetian one.

It was not until twenty years later, however, that she was able to do this. The Venetian doge at that time was blind eighty-year-old Enrico Dandolo—it is said that he had been blinded by the Byzantines and so hated them even more than most Venetians now did. When the Crusaders of the Fourth Crusade came to him and asked him to provide the shipping to take them to the Holy Land, he saw his chance.

"For eighty-five thousand marks," he said, "we will transport forty-five hundred horses, four thousand knights, nine thousand squires, and twenty thousand foot soldiers to the land of the Infidel. But it must be in cash paid down."

The Crusaders agreed to the terms, but after a long year of fruitless efforts, they still lacked thirty-four thousand marks.

"Well and good," said Dandolo. "But we must have something for our efforts. If you take Zara"—Zara on the Dalmatian coast, once Venetian, was now in the hands of the Hungarians—"we will forgive you this." When Zara was taken, he added Constantinople to the list of what he wanted.

Some of the Crusaders balked at this, but most of them were content and made no protest. The fleet sailed, but not to the Holy Land. It sailed toward the Bosporus.

In July, 1204, the Crusaders and the Venetians took the city. Although its greatest days had gone, it was still the richest city in Christendom and the booty may have been worth a hundred million modern dollars.

But Venice was not interested only in booty, although she pocketed her share of it. Nor was she much interested in pomp and circumstance. The Crusaders offered to make Dandolo the new Byzantine emperor, but he declined with thanks. Instead he asked for the best—or from the Venetian point of view, the most useful—parts of the Byzantine realm: every important seaport; every important commercial city; and every strong castle that controlled shipping routes.

These were handed over to him, and he then added a third title to his titles of Doge of Venice and Duke of Dalmatia—Despot and Lord of a Quarter and a Half of the Roman (i.e. Greek) Empire! This added up to three-eighths, but it was the only three-eighths that was worth having. For all practical purposes the Venetian Empire was the old Byzantine Empire with a new name.

Indeed, so completely Byzantine was Venice both in its territory and in many of its interests that in 1222 it was seriously proposed that the Venetian government be moved to Constantinople and set up in the old Byzantine capital.

In a tense meeting of the Great Council, speaker after speaker urged that Venice take this step, and it seemed likely that the idea would be carried out. But then one of the oldest and wisest of the councilors—his name was Angelo Faliero —rose to his feet and spoke:

"Do you want some future traveler to come to these lovely islands of ours and find the canals choked, the dikes leveled, and the houses ruined? Do you want some foreign provincial governor to sit in these halls and dictate his laws to a scanty and fever-stricken population in what was once great Venice?"

Immediately a vote was called for, and everyone held his breath as the results were tallied. It was 321 to 320 in favor of not moving. By one single vote, then, Venice had decided to stay where she was. This was ever afterward known as the Vote of Providence. Providence had moved the minds of enough men to keep Venice from doing a very foolish thing.

For foolish indeed it would have been. If Venice had moved to Constantinople, she would have become a second Byzantium and nothing more; nor, probably, could she have long outlasted the first Byzantium. It was only by staying in her lagoons that she could fulfill her destiny. It was only by staying where she was that she could create the first mighty maritime empire of modern times. (The next one, the British Empire, did not come into being until more than five hundred years later.) For in her lagoons, Venice was halfway between Europe, which was just beginning to be a place where one could buy and sell things at a profit, and Asia, which was the fabled source of splendid things to buy and sell. In her lagoons, Venice could do business with both of them. This she did.

But although this put Venice well on her way to becoming prosperous and mighty, her troubles were not by any means over.

First came a long war with her rival, Genoa. During the Middle Ages many of the Italian republics became important sea powers. Pisa was one, as was Ragusa (now Dubrovnik in Yugoslavia, and the place that gave us our word *argosy*, meaning a large and stately ship). So was Amalfi. Between 800 and 1100 that picturesque little city had fleets almost as large as Venice's and a rich and flourishing trade with North Africa.

But by the thirteenth century only Genoa and Venice were still important, and each thought the other should be eliminated. The war was fought to determine which it should be. It lasted for a hundred years, with victories going to both sides, and Venice only won it when Vettor Pisani, the Venetian admiral, was recalled from undeserved disgrace, and patriotically forgave the wrongs which had been done him. Once again in command, he sailed to Chioggia, twenty miles down the lagoon, and there he blockaded the Genoese fleet. After some weeks, the Genoese admiral surrendered. This was in June, 1380. Genoa never struck at Venice again.

Over and above this, Venice made the mistake of trying to be a land power. She had been warned against this by Tomaso Mocenigo, one of the wisest of her doges. On his deathbed in 1423, he told the Venetians that if Venice remained a sea power she would have all the gold in Christendom. "But if you move onto the mainland," he said, "you will live in a perpetual state of war. You will spend your fortune and your honor and live at the mercy of professional soldiers."

Unfortunately, the Venetians did not heed him. They listened instead to his successor, Francesco Foscari, who argued that Venice needed the cornlands and the vine-covered hills of northern Italy. The Venetians set out to win these. Beginning only two years after Mocenigo's death, they conquered city after city in northern Italy—Vicenza, Verona, Bergamo, Cremona, and many others. By the end of the century they had pushed their frontier almost to the gates of Milan.

But then, as Mocenigo had predicted, the enemies they had made combined against them. The League of Cambray was organized, and its members, France, Aragon, Germany, and Milan, urged on by Pope Julius II, swore that they would drive this greedy interloper back to the lagoons.

"I am going to make you a village of fishermen," the pope told the Venetians. And after they were defeated disastrously in the battle of Agnadello (1509), he almost did. It was only because he now began to fear his allies that he failed to crush Venice completely.

And there were other disasters: earthquakes, fires, and floods.

But in the long run Venice overcame them all, and as a result, the next three hundred and fifty years were days of a glory and a glittering splendor that has rarely been equaled and never surpassed anywhere, at any time.

An Empire Built by Trade

Venice was a splendor—and an empire—built by trade.

This does not mean that sea power—naval sea power—did not play an important part. Around 1890, an American admiral, Alfred Thayer Mahan, came to the conclusion that the only sure foundation for national greatness was control of the seas. He wrote many books and articles on the subject, and they made him world-famous. But the Venetians had found this out many centuries before Admiral Mahan was born. They knew that they were able to send their heavily-laden round ships and their great merchant galleys all over the world for "the honor and profit of the republic"—that is how the instructions to their captains read—only because their triremes, their *gatti* (large war galleys rowed by two hundred oarsmen), and their *fuste, galeotte, bregantini,* and *fregate* (light, swift cruisers) had swept the waters clear of every possible enemy. And the honor which they had won by sending their stately vessels all over the world had brought so much profit that the city built on a sand bank and piles became not only the largest in Europe but one of the wealthiest in the world.

"The population of Venice is now one hundred and ninety thousand," said Doge Tomaso Mocenigo in his deathbed statement, "and of these, three thousand are employed in the silk industry, and sixteen thousand in the wool industry. Between shipwrights, caulkers, and riggers, the arsenal employs seventeen thousand men. At least twenty-five thousand Venetians go to sea as sailors. Her merchant marine numbers three thousand vessels, and her navy three hundred. She constructs forty-five galleys a year."

But that was only part of the story.

"The value of her houses and palaces," he continued, "is seven million ducats, and over and above this she coins one million gold ducats a year as well as another million *grossi* (silver ducats)."

Florence alone, said Doge Mocenigo, bought eight hundred and forty thousand ducats' worth of merchandise from Venice annually, and Florence, although the most important of them, was only one of Venice's many customers. For Venice traded everywhere.

"The wines of Venice," the poet Petrarch wrote a friend during the 1350s—he meant the wines carried in Venetian vessels—"sparkle in the glasses of Breton fishermen, and Venetian honey"—he meant the honey brought by Venetian traders—"is tasted in the houses of the Russians."

To be sure, he remarked, Venetian ships did not go further than Russia. They stopped at the Don River. But Venetian merchants did not. "They often continue their travels by land until they have crossed the Ganges and the Caucasus, and have come to India and China and the shores of the Eastern Ocean."

Not only wine and honey were exported by Venetians. Their outgoing vessels carried dried fruit, salt meat, salt fish, metal (especially iron), lumber (the Near East was almost treeless), fur, linen, hemp and hempen products, wool and woolen cloth—and slaves.

"Ye Venetians are inveterate slave traders!" cried a pope angrily. But neither he nor anyone else could stop them from selling unfortunate Christians (mostly Slavs) in the slave markets of Moslem Beirut and Moslem Cairo.

With the money thus earned, the Venetians brought back every kind of commodity. Among them they brought cloves, nutmeg, mace (nutmeg husks), ebony, sandalwood, camphor, and benzoin (an aromatic gum) from the Moluccas, Timor, Borneo, Sumatra, and Java, in Indonesia; aloes and rare woods from Cochin China (now South Vietnam); perfume, gums, spices, and silk from China and Japan; rubies from the Pegu Mountains in Burma; fine fabrics from Coramandel and Bengal; diamonds from Golconda (in India); pearls, sapphires, topazes, and cinnamon from Ceylon; lac, agates, brocades, and jewelry from Cambay (in Bombay); wrought arms, graven vessels, and embroidered shawls from India; bdelium (an acrid gum resin) from Sind (in Pakistan); musk from Tibet; galbanum (another gum resin) from Khurasan (in Iran); asafetida from Afghanistan; ambergris, civet, and ivory from Zanzibar; myrrh, balsam, and frankincense from Arabia.

They also imported pepper from the East Indies (pepper was the most profitable spice of all); gold from Tunis (but it was mined in the deepest of dark Africa); and cotton from Egypt (Alexander the Great is supposed to have discovered cotton in India, but the Venetians imported it from Egypt, and long-stapled Egyptian cotton is still as good as any in the world).

Ten million ducats in all! That was the total annual value of Venetian foreign trade during the sixteenth century. The annual profits were two million ducats. (In actual gold content, a ducat was worth just a little less than four American dollars, but in spending power it must have been worth at least ten. That means that the annual value of Venetian foreign trade was one hundred million dollars.)

More than one Venetian family had an annual income of two hundred thousand ducats and a family was not thought to be rich if it had less than twenty thousand. Yet there were many rich Venetian families. Indeed, it almost seemed as if Venice was like King Midas of the old fable. Everything she touched turned into gold.

Just as the city itself with its buildings and its towers rose from an empty salt marsh, so all of this wealth—and the trade that earned it—came from the smallest and most modest of beginnings.

Trade and barter are among the very oldest of human activities, and it is doubtful that there has ever been a people so primitive that it did not exchange the things it had too much of for the things it did not have. Even luxury trade goes back to prehistoric times. For example, long before Knossos, Tyre, or Rome, amber from the Baltic Sea was carried overland to Greece and Italy to be exchanged for precious goods from the south. But most trade began with things that were either necessary or thought to be necessary. It was so with Venetian trade.

During the Dark Ages in Europe, when the use of any kind of refrigeration was almost unknown, nothing was more important than salt. What with the backward state of agriculture and the raiding barbarians—and after the barbarians, the robber barons who followed them—it was not possible to keep swine and cattle fat enough to butcher except in summer, and without salt meat for winter use there would have been widespread starvation. (There was enough starvation as it was.) Furthermore, the Church forbade the use of meat on fast days, and the only practical substitute was fish. For the most part, it had to be salt fish.

Salt, therefore, was a precious commodity. And because of her position in the salt marshes, Venice had almost a monopoly on salt.

She took full advantage of this. As soon as her fleeing citizens had established themselves on their islands, their ships (they were mostly barges then) began moving up the nearby rivers with their gleaming cargo. Salt from Venice was shoveled onto the quays of Parma, Piacenza, Pavia, and even Milan. From there, some of it went to Germany and central Europe. Venetian salt and Venetian salt only! The Venetians saw to that; some of Venice's earliest wars were salt wars, waged against her neighbors—Comacchio, Ravenna, Rimini, and other cities on the Adriatic shore—in order to deprive them of even the smallest share in the profitable business.

But the salt trade was only the beginning. It was soon followed by trade in timber and then in wheat. Venice freighted oak and larch and fir from the forests in the mountains above her, and she freighted wheat from Apulia. Both trades flourished, and soon, encouraged by their success and by their growing reputation as seamen, the Venetians found themselves engaged in carrying every kind of cargo that could be loaded on a vessel. "Before 600, they had become a seafaring and a trading people," wrote the historian James Westfall Thompson.

This does not mean that the Venetians did not do some land trading too, and right from the beginning. As early as

630, for example, Italian merchants were plodding across the Alps with their mules and their bales of goods to take part in the fairs held by King Dagobert at St. Denis in France. Some of them were Venetians. In the 800s, Charlemagne, after he found out that he could not rule Venice, welcomed Venetian traders to France. Bowing and scraping in his presence, they offered him plumes from rare birds as well as rich cloth from Tyre, which was dyed, they said, a truly royal purple. In 830, they came to the court of Louis the Pious (Charlemagne's eldest son), who named some of his gold coins *venecias* in their honor. By 877, Venice had signed treaties with the Holy Roman emperors Lothair I and Ludwig II which allowed Venetian merchants to travel and to buy and sell anywhere in Germany—provided, of course, that they paid the established tolls.

Nevertheless, sea trading and seafaring were always more important to the Venetians, even though at first it was only what was called *cabotaggio*, or coastal trade. Almost as soon as there was a Venice, tubby little Venetian ships with a single lateen sail and a broad rudder (sort of an enlarged oar) hung on each quarter moved up and down the Adriatic Sea from one end to the other. Some of the more adventurous went to the Ionian islands off western Greece. In these voyages, the Venetians were aided by local knowledge. A northbound current flows along the coast of Dalmatia and a southbound current along the coast of Italy. They were able to use the one they needed.

Soon, however, even the Adriatic and Ionian seas were left behind, and by 750, Venetian ships and the men aboard them were familiar sights throughout the whole Mediterranean. They sailed to Marseilles and Barcelona and to North Africa. Obviously they sailed to Constantinople. The

Byzantine emperor was still their overlord. They were seen off Syria and Cyprus and Egypt. Alexandria was almost a home port.

But even these voyages that went so far and wide were just longer coastal voyages. The compass was then known only to the Chinese, and there were few, if any, other navigating instruments. As much as they could, in these early days, the Venetians made their voyages from headland to headland. They were hardly ever out of sight of land.

Even this was possible only because the officers and crewmen on these ships were all Venetian citizens (slaves were not used even to tug the oars until the sixteenth century), and every Venetian was a born sailor. Every Venetian knew how to handle a vessel; and he was so familiar with the seacoasts, islands, and ports the Venetians sailed to that the captain could call on him for advice. A Venetian sailor also spoke the language of every country the Venetians visited, as well as the so-called *lingua franca* of the eastern Mediterranean. The latter was a hodgepodge of Italian, Provençal, French, and other languages, invented by the sailors, and whoever spoke it could do business wherever he went.

Even in those days the voyages to the Near East—to Syria and Egypt—were the most important, and it was from the Near East that one day in 828 a Venetian ship brought back to Venice a very special cargo. It was more precious to them than all the apes and ivory and peacocks, the gold and pepper and perfumes that they had ever carried.

"In those days"—again it is Martino da Canale who speaks—"a Venetian ship came to Alexandria—this is the city in which Messer San Marco was martyred and buried— and aboard this ship were three Venetians, Messer Rustico of Torcello, Messer Buono of Malamocco, and one Stauricio, and when they learned that the saint's body was there, they longed greatly to bring it back to Venice.

"They went, therefore, to one of the guardians of the saint's tomb, and said to him: 'If you let us take the body of St. Mark back to Venice, we will make you a very rich man.'

"But he was afraid, and replied thus: 'The heathen here revere him as much as you do. They would cut off my head.'

" 'That may be as you say,' they answered. 'But we will wait here, for we know that the blessed Evangelist will command you to bring him.'

"And so it came about, for somewhat later this guardian went to the three Venetians and told them he would help them remove the body if they told him how.

" 'In this manner,' they replied. 'Take him from his tomb, and put him in a casket, and cover him with cabbages and hog meat, and then bury another body in his place so that the people will not know that he is gone.' This they instructed him because they knew that the Moslems would not touch pork.

"This the guardian did, and the three Venetians put the body of the saint into a basket and carried it to their ship, where they hoisted it to a yardarm.

"But thereupon a sweet scent drifted through the city and the men of Alexandria knew the saint was being taken. They hastened to the ship only to see the basket swinging there.

" '*Hanzir! Hanzir!* (Hog meat! Hog meat!)' they shouted and fled in panic."

That was not quite the end of the story. The ship sailed on a fair wind, but when it reached the coast of Greece there was a terrible storm. The Venetians were sleeping, and the ship with its precious cargo would have been lost had the saint not wakened them. A year after they left Alexandria, they sailed into Venice, and soon St. Mark was made the patron saint of the city.

Thus an old prophecy was fulfilled. For according to an ancient story, Mark the Evangelist had once been almost shipwrecked off the Venetian shore. All at once Christ had appeared and calmed the tempest's fury. Then he had turned to St. Mark. "*Pax tibi, evangelista mea!* Peace to thee, my evangelist!" he had said. And he had promised that Mark's final resting place would be Venice.

Now it was, and the Venetians built the magnificent Church of St. Mark's to house his tomb. Furthermore, a lion holding an open book with Christ's words written upon it— the lion was the saint's symbol—was placed upon the scarlet and golden banner of the republic. And from then on the Venetians fought and traded under the Lion of St. Mark.

The Venetians were able to build this church and honor their saint in this way because even at that early date, when most of Europe was a wild woodland, and when London and Paris were collections of hovels, and Rome with its ruins was deserted except for bandit lords and their retainers, Venice had already taken the first steps toward becoming "a warehouse and a city and a seaport and a fortress."

The Venetians were proud of this, and proud that they had made it so. They were proud to be merchant princes, or even just plain merchants. In this respect, they were unlike the Byzantines who had been their masters.

One of their Byzantine overlords once looked out of his palace window and saw, tied to the quay below him, a ship that was said to belong to his wife. He flew into a rage.

"You made me your holy emperor," he cried, "and now I am degraded into a tradesman."

In contrast, Doge Giustiniano Partecipazio—it was he

who ruled when St. Mark was brought from Egypt—did not conceal his commercial activities. And he was successful in them. One of his legacies was twelve hundred silver *libbre* (pounds)—"provided that the ship and cargo in which they are invested returns safely." A relative, Bishop Orso Parteci-pazio, left a sack of pepper. Not even his sacred vestments kept him from making an honest ducat when he could.

But though high and low bought and sold—and some of both classes grew wealthy—Venetian commerce was still relatively small at this early time (between 800 and 1000), and was still almost all in private hands. The state-owned arsenal—it got its name from the Arabic *daar senaah*, or place of work—would not be founded until 1104, and until then all ships were built in private shipyards called *squeri*. They are still called *squeri* today, but most of them are now used only to build gondolas. Generally speaking, ships sailed wherever their owners wanted them to—which was wherever they could find business worth their trouble.

But after the year 1000—and especially after the conquest of Constantinople in 1204—all this changed completely. "Once," wrote the English poet William Wordsworth, speaking of Venice, "did she hold the gorgeous East in fee." After Constantinople fell, Venice indeed did—and the West too! And certainly her commerce could no longer be called small. It blossomed and grew until no one had ever seen anything like it before. The *fondamenta* (quays) were piled higher and higher with goods that were ever more precious, and commerce became so important to Venice that she could no longer leave it in individual hands.

Private enterprise was allowed to continue. Indeed, it was encouraged, and this is the most notable thing about Vene-tian commerce at the time it reached its peak. But every day and every year, this private enterprise was more and more controlled by the state. Venetian noblemen—and citizens, the next lower class—were allowed to organize *fraterne* (partnerships or brotherhoods), *colleganze* (companies in which anyone, rich or poor, could invest, and which lasted only for the duration of a single voyage), and other associations. But when they did so, they had to abide by the rules. A committee, the *savii alla mercanzia* (merchant-marine councilors) saw to it that they did.

These rules covered almost everything.

One important rule in the great days of Venetian commerce was that all merchant vessels had to sail in convoys, which the Venetians called "caravans."

There were six of these convoys—or perhaps we should say convoy routes, since some places were visited by more than one Venetian convoy each year. One of them went to Constantinople and to "Romania" (what was left of the old Byzantine Empire); one to Alexandria; one to Syria; one to the Tana River and the Black Sea; one to North Africa; and one to England and Flanders.

Usually, the convoys left Venice just before the winter storms had begun, or just after they were over. They tried to return at Easter, or in September, or at Christmas— in time for the Rialto fairs.

Most of the ships in these convoys were owned by Venice itself, which built them with assembly-line methods long before the phrase "assembly line" was ever heard of, and chartered them to the highest bidder. Not only the ships, but their equipment too was standardized. This simplified repairs and the replacement of parts, particularly when ships were far from home.

The state also saw to it that ships were both safe and

sound. A century ago, an English merchant, Samuel Plimsoll, persuaded the British Parliament to pass a law which required shipowners to paint a mark on the water line of all vessels to show the limit to which they could be safely loaded. This is still known as the Plimsoll mark. But many centuries before Samuel Plimsoll, the Venetians did the same. They painted a cross on their ships for the same purpose.

In their great days, the Venetians took all the pains they could to make sure that their ships were well designed. The *proti* (foremen), who were the naval architects of the time, were well treated and well paid, and their work was by no means limited to laying down the lines. From the cutting of timber in the forest to the final launching, the *proti* were in charge of every detail. Nor were the Venetians afraid to experiment. One of the most famous of Venetian ship designers was Vettor Fausto, a poor Greek scholar who read Hesiod and Homer and lectured on Greek rhetoric. He had read the scientist Archimedes too, and in 1529 he decided to try to build a quinquereme, the largest vessel of the ancient Romans. He was successful and his vessel outraced the swiftest light galley in the Venetian navy. But it was extremely expensive and no more were constructed.

In addition the state gave much thought to the well-being of its crews. As far back as 1476, it permitted the formation of the Guild of St. Nicholas. St. Nicholas was the patron saint of seamen, and the guild was the forerunner of the modern seamen's union. Even the slaves—when slaves were finally used—were well cared for. The owner had to provide each one with the prescribed food, two shirts, two pairs of linen drawers, a coat of red, green, or blue, and a woolen *gabbano* (sleeveless cloak) for cold or stormy weather.

It was a fine thing to see one of the Venetian convoys set sail. Often it was made up of ten or more cogs (broad-beamed merchant ships) and galleys. Besides its cargo, each vessel carried wine, salted meat, oil, vinegar, sausages, beans, biscuits, and bread, as well as drugs in case of need. It also carried a band, which by law could not consist of less than two timbrels, one drum, two trumpets, and some kettledrums. As the ships were warped into the channel, these sounded loudly while the officers, distinguished passengers, and such of the sailors as were not handling the oars or sheets lined the rail. Those on shore saw them off with high hopes, but knew too that these hopes might not be realized, for seafaring was hazardous in those days, and not every husband, brother, and son returned.

The Republic of Venice did one thing more for its merchants: It provided them with reliable money. In 1284, the first gold ducat was coined. It was of metal "as fine or finer than the gold used in the Florentine florin." Because it was never devalued, it gained world-wide circulation, and in the eastern Mediterranean, it became the principal coin of commerce. It was well known even in England.

"My daughter and my ducats!" cries Shylock in *The Merchant of Venice*. Everyone knows what he means.

The Venetians also invented the letter of credit. A merchant no longer had to carry heavy sacks of coin which could be stolen or lost at sea. A letter from his head office in Venice to its foreign agent would get him all the coin he needed.

Once, in an emergency, the Venetians even used leather money. In 1118, while fighting before Tyre, the doge did not have any gold with which to pay his men-at-arms and sailors. He gave them strips of leather. Each could be redeemed for five gold ducats in Venice.

To pay for a war with the Byzantines, the Venetians floated the first public bond issue in Europe. The bonds paid 4 per cent interest and were sold as well as bought. They helped Venetian foreign trade, for foreign merchants, and even kings and princes, wanted them, and so they could be used to pay for purchases or to pay off debts. And their price did not fall; it soared.

Thus equipped, the Venetians went to all the places already mentioned—and to a few more. They went to Cairo by the ancient Nile. Like Alexandria, Cairo was "the market place of the two worlds," the terminus of a trade route which began in India. Cargo loaded there was taken boldly across the Arabian Sea to Aden, then brought by Egyptian seamen to Adab on the Egyptian Red Sea coast. From Adab it was carried overland to the Nile and then floated down the river to its destination in low, flat boats. In the spring one could buy in Cairo goods which had been produced in Peking or Ceylon the autumn before.

The Venetians went to Damascus, another terminus of Indian trade. This route brought goods overseas to Hormuz on the Persian Gulf and then to Baghdad. The Venetians also went to Trebizond on the Black Sea, where camel trains came snarling in from Samarkand and Tashkent and Bukhara in Central Asia. And they went to Tunis, to foggy London, and, of course, to Bruges in the Low Countries. Bruges, with its own network of bridges and canals, and with its own rich merchants, was often called "the northern Venice." It traded heavily with the southern Venice.

For some Venetian merchants these places were only the beginning. For most, the Flanders voyage was enough, as it meant sailing up the long Spanish and Portuguese coast swept by huge Atlantic rollers, and then crossing the stormy Bay of Biscay. But to Vivaldo and Ugolino de' Vivaldi, two Venetian shipbuilders, the Atlantic was a challenge. Long before Columbus, they sailed westward and southward, "so that by way of the Ocean Sea," they might come to India. They were seen sailing past Cape Juby on the west coast of Africa, but were never heard of again.

Toward the East too, distance and the unknown presented a challenge, and in 1338 six Venetian merchants organized a Delhi company and set out overland for India. They crossed the Volga at Astrakhan at the north end of the Caspian Sea; then the fabled Amu Darya (Alexander called it the Oxus); and finally they reached the lofty Pamir Mountains. Hardly one of these was less than twenty thousand feet high, but the merchants struggled through the ice and snow with high hopes. The ruler of Delhi, Mohammed el Tughlak, was one of the cruelest monarchs who ever lived, but although he flayed rivals to his throne alive—and did other things even worse—he was generous to strangers. He was generous to the six Venetians. Because they had come so far, he gave them two hundred thousand gold bezants. Most of these they invested in pearls, which were small and easy to carry. But even at that, the voyage was so long and the expenses of it so great that they hardly made a profit.

The most famous of all Venetian merchant-travelers went eastward too. He lived between the days of the Vivaldi and the time of the six men who went to Delhi. He was Marco Polo, who was born almost within sight of the Rialto Bridge in Venice in 1254, and died there in 1324.

"Since the days when our Lord God did create the first father, Adam," wrote a man who lived in Marco Polo's day and age, "there has been no man, either Christian or pagan or of any other people, who has seen and searched into so much of the world and its marvels as this man has."

Marco was a long, gangling, curious, reddish-haired boy of seventeen when his adventures began. He had been born while his father, Niccolo, and his uncle, Matteo, were deep in Asia. When they decided to return there in 1271—they had promised Kublai Khan to bring him Christian priests and a message from the pope—they took Marco with them.

The journey was a long difficult one, and it took several years to make. For in order to get to Cathay, they had to cross all of Central Asia, including the great Gobi Desert, where they nearly perished. (They thought the dry winds they heard howling were dervishes and devils.) But finally, they reached Kanbaligh (the Xanadu of the poem by Coleridge, and our Peking), where Kublai received them with great joy. He was particularly pleased with young Marco. He attached him to his civil service, sent him on long voyages, and at one time made him governor of the enormous city of Yangchow.

But fortunately for us, Marco was often homesick and he continually asked Kublai to let him return to Venice. At first, the mighty Mongol monarch refused. But as Kublai grew older, he began to realize that when he died his successor might not treat the Venetian as well as he had, and finally, in 1292, he allowed him to depart. Marco was put in charge of a mission to conduct a Chinese princess to Persia, where she was to marry Kublai's grandnephew.

He went there in state by way of Sumatra and Ceylon, and when he reached Persia he learned that Kublai was dead. This left him free and he went on to Venice. After three years of journeying, he arrived in rags, but sewed into them were gems of such value that not even the Venetians had ever seen their like. After that, he was always known as Marco Millions.

He had planned to settle down, but war broke out with Genoa, and in 1299 he served as an officer on a Venetian galley. It was captured by the Genoese, and off he went to Genoa as a prisoner. It was lucky for the whole world that he did, for in prison he dictated his *Book of Marvels* to a fellow captive. It is now known as *The Travels of Marco Polo*. Although most people of his time thought him a great liar, his book is one of the most wonderful ever written. In it, he tells of many marvelous things, and we now know he really did see most of them. He speaks of rock that burns (coal), paper, gunpowder, and printing. (The Chinese had all these long before the Western world ever thought of them.) He describes the great city of Hankow with its twelve thousand bridges. He even tells of distant "Cipango." Today we know Cipango was Japan.

Finally, he speaks of the eastern ocean. It is the same ocean as the western ocean, he insists. This would be remembered at the court of Ferdinand and Isabella two hundred years later, when Columbus came begging for help.

Yet even at that, Venice did not owe her commercial greatness to travelers like Marco Polo, or seafarers like the Vivaldi, or the six who crossed the mountains to India. She owed it instead to merchants of a much more modest and everyday sort. These merchants did sometimes travel—but almost always only in their youth. For the most part, they stayed close to their palaces and places of business, trying to manage their affairs so that each year their ledgers would leave them in the black.

What were these merchants like? How did they do their business and how did they learn to do it? What were their problems and how did they solve them?

Fortunately, an American scholar, Frederic Chapin Lane, has written a very careful study of the life of just one of these merchants of Venice. But he was a typical merchant of Venice, and from him we can learn all we need to know.

A
Merchant of
Venice

The merchant's name was Andrea Barbarigo, and he was a member of an ancient and noble family which had lived in Venice for as long as there had been a Venice in which to live. It was also a very wealthy family. Little Andrea was born—probably in 1399—with a gold spoon in his mouth.

But like many another Venetian family, the Barbarigi were suddenly brought face to face with disaster—and what made it worse, this was because Andrea's father, Niccolo Barbarigo, had flagrantly neglected his duty.

In those days, the galleys which plied between Venice and Alexandria carried just about the richest cargoes of all. They took out great sacks of gold and silver, and they brought back the spices of the Indies, which were worth their weight in either of these precious metals.

This voyage was as difficult and dangerous as any. The Venetians had to stay in Egypt late enough into the fall for the Indian Ocean monsoons to carry the cargo they were seeking from India to the land of the Pharaohs. Then they had to hasten to Venice as swiftly as possible so as to reach the city in time for the Christmas fairs. In order to do this, they often disobeyed orders from the state and sailed through the narrow channels between the long chain of Dalmatian islands and the rugged Dalmatian coast—even though this meant struggling against the *bora* (the savage winter north wind).

In 1417, Niccolo Barbarigo did just this. He was not only captain of his own ship but commander of the Alexandria fleet, and, disregarding both common sense and instructions, he led it between island and island and between island and shore. He even sailed at night, although this was against regulations too.

He almost reached his destination. But as his fleet came out of the Zara channel—more than halfway up the Dalmatian coast—a sudden storm struck it, and in the bleak darkness, one of the galleys was driven ashore on a rocky island called Ulbo.

The ship's crew promptly lit flares. But although Niccolo's flagship was not more than a hundred yards away, he made no effort to save the wrecked vessel. Instead, he kept on sailing until he had made a safe port. Only then did he send back a ship's boat to see what could be done. He himself continued on to Venice. Either he was afraid of wrecking his own vessel too—this is what his friends argued —or he wanted to reach the market ahead of the other vessels. No one knows.

The Venetian government did not care. As far as they were concerned, he had plainly and flagrantly disobeyed their rules, and then left a Venetian ship—and the Venetians aboard it—to the mercies of the sea. He was immediately relieved of his command, tried and convicted, and fined the enormous sum of ten thousand ducats. He was lucky that that was all.

Niccolo was not only disgraced; he was ruined, and the Barbarigi were ruined too. Or to speak more accurately, they were *almost* ruined. For there was still Niccolo's son, who was now eighteen years old.

There was something in Andrea that set him apart from the growing numbers of young noblemen who had failed in business and who had nothing left but their haughty manners and their proud names. Andrea's father had fallen, but he, the son, would rise again. He would do so by starting from the very bottom, as a young Venetian nobleman was supposed to do.

He wasted little or no time in getting started. In 1418— the year following his father's fall from grace—he stepped aboard a Venetian ship. He had signed on as a bowman of the quarter-deck.

Supposedly he was just that. Supposedly he was one of the ship's archers—an enrolled soldier in the military contingent carried by every Venetian galley to protect it from attack whether by pirate or by open enemy. But actually the military role of these young gentlemen who called themselves bowmen of the quarter-deck was not important. Most of the fighting was done by the common bowmen.

The real business of a bowman of the quarter-deck was to learn the principles of seafaring and commerce. Andrea was an apprentice merchant, not an apprentice fighting man. He ate in the captain's mess, and there he was supposed to listen to the ship's officers, who knew every seaport, and to the older merchants, who had engaged in trade in almost all of them. To listen and to remember what he heard. For doing this—and for performing such small services as might be asked of him—the bowman of the quarter-deck was paid a nominal wage and given his keep. He also had the right to load a small amount of cargo without paying any freight.

The latter privilege was especially useful to Andrea. In his disgrace, his father had become a monk—Fra Niccolo of the Brothers of Charity—and could not help him. But Andrea's mother, who was of the even nobler Faliero family, was able to give him two hundred ducats.

This he invested wisely in goods which brought him a profit. Thus he was earning while he was learning—earning as he watched the older merchants bargain and haggle down to the last penny on the quays of Alexandria, or as he discussed wine and kermes dye and cheeses with his rich uncles and cousins, who were landholders with large estates in Crete.

But Andrea Barbarigo did not stay at sea forever or even for long. While he was still in his twenties, the government of Venice appointed him one of the official attorneys attached to what was called the Court of Petition. This was the court in which all commercial cases were heard, and the official attorneys there were usually young men who were still studying law.

The court was another good place in which to gain experience and to learn about the practices of trade. It was also a good place in which to make influential friends. Almost every important businessman in Venice appeared before the court sooner or later, and although he almost always brought along his own lawyer, one of the official attorneys was always assigned to him too. If the latter made a good impression, it was not forgotten.

Young Andrea served in this court for about five years, but even while he served there he also had some formal instruction from professional schoolteachers. Possibly at night, and certainly in his spare time, he studied arithmetic and double-entry bookkeeping from one of the many Venetian "masters of the abacus"—the abacus, a medieval counting device, is still used in China. One of Andrea's account books shows that he also paid thirteen ducats to a Messer Piero de la Memoria for teaching him how to remember things. Memory was very important in those days, especially for a would-be merchant. There were no newspapers with their financial pages, and the only way one could keep track of the ups and downs of prices was to listen carefully on the Rialto and remember everything he heard.

When Andrea finally set himself up in business, he was thirty-two years old. The first entry in his ledger shows that he was then worth sixteen hundred ducats. But that was not enough for the ventures he planned, and so he raised further capital by selling the government bonds he owned—in Venice one was obliged to buy government bonds but not to keep them—and by selling those of his mother; by subletting part of the palace which, to save money, he had rented instead of buying; by dispensing with owning a slave and hiring one instead; and finally, by borrowing some cash.

Andrea, like other Venetian merchants, was always borrowing money. He could not have stayed in business without doing this. Once, when he had ten thousand ducats invested in cargoes bound for England and Egypt, he had to pawn a ring to get ten ducats for household expenses!

Thus Andrea started out with trading funds of thirty-three hundred ducats. Seventeen years later he died at the age of forty-nine and left a business worth fifteen thousand ducats. To be sure, this did not make him a truly wealthy man. But he had multiplied by seventy-five the two hundred ducats his mother had given him in 1418; and in the meanwhile he had supported his mother, partly supported an aging mother-in-law, brought up two sons, and still had enough money left over to live magnificently, and even to buy a villa on the mainland where he could spend his summers!

How did he manage to do all this?

How did the impoverished apprentice whose hopes were shattered when his father's misdeed was punished become one of those portly signors and rich burghers with which Venice was filled? How did young Andrea with his slender resources become Messer Andrea Barbarigo, merchant of Venice?

We should try to find out, for if we know the answer, we will know what made Venice the leader in the commercial revolution that ushered Europe out of the Dark Ages and into modern times.

A businessman, Professor Lane suggests, is one who seeks to make a profit by calculating the results of buying and selling. Andrea Barbarigo rescued his family from their ruin and made his modest fortune by doing just this. Seated like a watchful spider in his home and place of business on the Grand Canal he spent most of his waking hours considering what things to buy and what to sell.

Should he invest in Syrian cotton, or in spices at Alexandria? Should he import wine from Crete, or wheat from southern Italy? Should he do business in English cloth, Spanish wool and olive oil, or Palermo sugar? And when?

In 1430, for example—that was before he had set up in business on his own—he shipped six bales of pepper to Bruges, and it was sold there. The vessel then returned by way of London, where it picked up twenty-three barrels of tin and pewter ware and twenty-three lengths of fine English cloth. The voyage was a long one, but even at that, and even though he had to pay tribute to a Spanish admiral off Sicily—the admiral asked for jewels but Andrea's Venetian captain pawned off glass beads on him—he made enough on the two transactions to pay all his expenses with something left over to reinvest.

But suppose everyone had shipped pepper to Bruges and it had all been piled up in the warehouses at the same time. Suppose everyone had brought back English pewter and English cloth. Andrea might easily have been ruined.

On another trip to and from Bruges, there was no return cargo available. What did Andrea do? He invested in a share of the ship's ballast. This was rock sand or sand—and he sold it to the Murano glassmakers.

In a third venture—and, of course, Andrea engaged in many, many more—he had his agents search the mountains of the Abruzzi (in central Italy) for a kind of cheap goatskin called *albertoni*. He would ship these skins to northern Europe, where the climate was cold, and where rare fur was becoming too expensive for any except the very rich.

"Buy me twenty-five thousand weights," he wrote. "But only if the price is right. Otherwise send back the money. Do not invest it in wheat."

The price wasn't right, but his agents seem to have bought anyway. He cut his losses, however, by shipping the skins to Flanders as quickly as he could, and then circulating the report that the next year's skins were going to be even more expensive and of very poor quality.

And so Andrea continued to do well. He owed his success in part to the sharp business skill he always showed. But he owed it also to his associates, for then as now a business-man did not operate alone.

First of all, he took great pains to befriend a big merchant. The man he chose was Francesco Balbi. Balbi was fourteen years older than Andrea—Andrea had probably gained his good will when he was attached to the Court of Petition—

and at a time when most banking was dominated by the Medici of Florence, he was one of the three or four bankers in Venice.

This friendship was very important to Andrea. On the practical side, he could always go to Balbi when he needed credit. Balbi would then either permit him to overdraw his account; or buy his bills of exchange; or take over Andrea's claims against someone who had purchased goods from Andrea and had not paid for them. The banker made money on these transactions, but so did Andrea, although not as much. More important, however, was the fact that the great banker had confidence in Andrea. That meant that all the other businessmen of Venice could have confidence in him too.

Andrea also had good luck, or showed good judgment, in his choice of partners. Among his first partners were three brothers: Vittore, Alban, and Giovanni Cappello. It was to them that he had sold his Bruges pepper. All three had traded far and wide, and Alban and Vittore had commanded vessels in the Flanders convoy. Alban later became a member of the doge's council. Vittore became Captain General of the Venetian war fleet, and in this capacity, he went down in Venetian history.

The Venetians were fighting the Turks, and the doge, Cristoforo Moro, was ordered to sail with the fleet. Hobbling to show his condition, Doge Moro appeared before the Great Council.

"I have had little experience at sea," he said in a high voice. "I am too old and find it hard to get about."

Vittore, a member of the council, arose. "You are needed, and you will go," he said calmly.

Only in Venice could a merchant talk to his prince that way. But in Venice a merchant was a prince too.

The Cappello brothers brought Andrea experience in trading and firsthand information about one of the most important trade centers. They brought him influence in government circles. They also brought him further funds to trade with, for in 1439 Andrea married their sister, Cristina Cappello, with a dowry of four thousand ducats. Needless to say, he put these where they could make more.

Andrea had other partners too, among them two cousins of the famous Cadamosto family. In the beginning, both of them—Alvise and Andrea—were content to sail to North Africa on Andrea Barbarigo's behalf with cloth, copper, spices, cotton, and red fezzes, which were exchanged for silks and for the gold Venice needed for its ducats. Andrea Cadamosto was happy to continue with this Barbary trade for the rest of his life. But Alvise wanted more. He decided to become an explorer as well as a merchant, and struck out for Africa on a swift caravel. There he pushed up many a crocodile-filled river, visited the straw-hut palace of King Bodumel of the Senegal, saw wild elephants and "fish horses" (hippopotami), and finally sailed up the Gambia River, where truly savage tribesmen drove him off, saying that his sailors were probably cannibals. On a second voyage, he discovered the Cape Verde Islands. But although he brought home a little gold as well as some gaudy native cotton goods and one hundred and fifty yellow and green parrots, which he sold for almost a ducat each, he did not find the rich cargoes he had hoped for.

Financially, he might have fared better if he had stayed with Barbarigo.

Andrea Barbarigo also saw to it that he had foreign agents who knew their business. In those days, this was even more important than it is now, for at a time when there was neither cable, telephone, or radio, and when ships were dependent either on the wind or on oar power, the agent of a Venetian merchant was often out of touch with his home office for weeks or even months at a time. A merchant's agent, then, had to be someone he could trust.

"If you don't trust a man," ran an old Venetian saying, "don't employ him. But if you do employ him, you must always trust him."

Andrea did not always live up to this adage. He had an agent in Syria whom he did not trust completely. But this agent, Alberto Dolceto, might have felt the same way about Andrea, for Andrea sometimes did business with another agent behind Alberto's back—and then told the second agent to be sure not to let Alberto know a thing about it.

The agent also had to be intelligent enough to make his own decisions. Usually his instructions from the home office were very specific, but sometimes they were out of date when they reached him. He had to know when to pay no attention to them as well as when to obey them.

Besides this, the agent had to know all about local conditions and local standards. In Spain, for example, the weights and measures were different from those in Venice. The agent had to know how to change Spanish weights and measures into Venetian ones without losing money in the process.

He also had to know how to secure shipping space. This was particularly difficult for a small merchant who did not own or charter his own vessel. The best way of doing it was to keep in the good graces of some big merchant. Often— in fact, usually—the agent accomplished this by using his connections to do the big merchant favors.

Finally, the agent had to be willing to take all this trouble for a small commission. It was never more than 1 or 2 per cent. But then, it was his employer, not he, who took the risks.

Andrea Barbarigo started out with modest means, but even the sons of rich merchants often had to start out in much the same way. We know about one of them, another Andrea—Andrea Sanudo. He made his first voyage in 1475. He went to Alexandria, and with him went a letter from his older brother, Benedetto.

"I commend you to God," Benedetto wrote, "and I pray to Him that you have a safe and prosperous journey."

But Andrea could do this, the letter continued, only if he took certain precautions. First, the young man must ever be careful of his health, and second, he must remember that he was under the orders of the vessel's captain. "Take care not to do anything he does not wish. Go wherever he goes. And above all, never absent yourself from the galley without his permission."

Be civil to your associates, Benedetto instructed his brother. They are all just as noble as you—even if their purses are not as full. If they are older than you, he said, address them with reverence.

He advised Andrea to take care of his spiritual needs. "The chaplain is Messer Piero Antoni. Make him your companion and always confer with him when you have a problem. He will always help you more than anyone else."

You will have a servant—one Pietro, Benedetto wrote. "His duty is to look after you and to take care of your belongings. Treat him with as much kindness as you can and be sure to give him a present whenever you leave the ship or come back to it. But keep the keys of your sea chest and your writing case in your own hands. Only give them to him when you send him to get something."

Beware of professional gamblers, he warned. "There will be some aboard who make the voyage only to play cards or backgammon, and if you lose a penny to them, they will swear that you have lost a ducat. So while others gamble, read one of the books you have with you, and if you tire of this and must play for your amusement, try a game of checkers with the chaplain."

As to shore leave, he said, "when the galley touches at some port, do not go too far from the quay, for when the drum beats, all must return to the ship at once. Those who do not, are left behind."

At Corfu and Crete, there was another danger. "Beware of the beautiful young ladies who haunt those islands." They would surely get his ducats if the gamblers hadn't.

Finally, when Andrea got to Alexandria, he must not fail to pay a formal call on the Venetian consul, and if he was invited, he could dine and spend the night with him. But only if he wanted to, and he might not, for some people said that the air of the city was fever-ridden and unhealthy. "But if you do return to the ship," his brother cautioned, "be sure you have someone with you, for the Arabs of the place are highhanded and insolent, but they will only molest you if you are alone."

That much for Andrea Sanudo's well-being, but brother Benedetto did not forget business: "Make sure you sell the hundred and ninety dozen red caps (fezzes such as those the Cadamostos took to Tunis) which I have sent to you. Buy pepper with the proceeds. Make sure it is good pepper even if you have to pay a ducat or two more than current price. If you then have any money left, buy sugar. If you can't get enough sugar, buy nutmegs. But be careful about buying nutmegs. Only buy them if you have to. A large supply is expected in from Syria, and I do not want to be overstocked."

Andrea Sanudo had goods worth thirty-five hundred ducats to trade with—not Andrea Barbarigo's mere two hundred—and it is probable that the seven other young noblemen employed by the house of Benedetto Sanudo & Co., and the *magnifico Capitano* as he was called (he was also on the Sanudo payroll), and the *padrone* (business manager of the whole affair) had like amounts. That made at least thirty-five thousand ducats in all, and these were supposed to be laid out on goods which could be brought back to Venice. There they could be sold at high prices—so high, in fact, that the merchants would make a substantial profit even after paying the expenses of the voyage, as well as the exit dues which had to be paid upon setting out and the duty to be paid upon return.

This they did, and the house of Sanudo & Co. flourished. So too did the hundred and fifty merchants on a convoy which in July, 1443, left Venice for Beirut and Alexandria carrying four hundred and sixty thousand ducats in cash and enough assorted goods to bring the total to a million ducats.

So did the wife who asked her husband to invest the hundred ducats she had saved up from her household money. So did the nurse who had put her savings into the hands of the baby she had brought up and who now had ships of his own. So did the humble gondolier who, after listening to the talk of the men he ferried, did not hesitate to put out some of the copper coins he had earned on ships and cargoes.

So, too, did another merchant who was even sharper than those already mentioned. "If, with the correspondence I send you," he wrote an agent, "there are also letters addressed to other agents, be sure to read your own letters first, and if they advise you to buy this kind of merchandise or sell that kind, go to a broker and do what the letters tell you to. Only then, distribute the other letters."

All is fair in competition.

With the possible exception of young Sanudo and his shipmates, none of the merchants we have talked about made huge profits or in themselves contributed greatly to the total Venetian wealth. But things add up, and out of the relatively modest ventures of men like Andrea Barbarigo, and the pittances invested by housewife, gondolier, and ancient nurse—these and the huge profits of a few big merchants—did indeed come the mighty ocean of Venetian prosperity, which was like nothing else in the world.

A
Government by
the Few but
for the Many

The grandeur and the glory of Venice grew out of something more than the business ability and talent for trading possessed by the descendants of the onetime Marsh Gauls. They had another quality of equal importance.

Almost more than any other people before or since, the Venetians believed firmly that government and business ought to, and must, go hand in hand. And so they deliberately set about to create a Venetian government that would serve the interests of Venetian business. For they firmly believed that what was good for Sanudo & Co.—or for Andrea Babarigo and his associates or for any other Venetian merchant, big or small—was good for Venice. And in many ways, this was true.

This government was not like any other of its day and age, and indeed the only government which can be compared with it is the government of England during the great days of its overseas adventures, which began just before the reign of Elizabeth and lasted well into the last century.

During that period, the lords of England—the nobly-born

lords of England, and some who became nobles because of the wealth they had amassed—organized company after company. The Muscovy Company, for trade with Russia. The Turkey or Levant Company, for trade with the Near East. The Hudson's Bay Company. The East India Company.

In these companies, the noble lords traded in everything from rare and costly furs to precious East Indian pearls, and because they could only begin operating when the government granted them a charter, and keep operating when it protected them, they made every effort to control the government. But this was not too hard to do. It was only necessary to make certain that the king—or his prime minister—had a large and profitable block of stock.

The Venetian noble lords did much the same—the Venetian noble *merchant* lords. But they did not control the government: they *were* the government. They owned it, lock, stock, and barrel, just as they owned one of their own companies, partnerships, or associations.

This government was one which the Venetians had worked out themselves—and over a long period of time.

As law and order returned to Italy after the Dark Ages and the barbarian invasions, most Italian cities and states had one of two forms of government. The first was a dictatorship. A warrior rode in at the head of his bands and had himself elected captain of the people. Once established, he refused to step down and ruled despotically. This was the kind of government that existed in Milan, and in Verona, and in many other places, particularly in the north.

The other was a rough, homespun merchant democracy which the citizens put together themselves. This kind of government was to be found in Florence, and in Siena, and in a number of small towns such as San Gimignano. It was not a true democracy as we understand the word today. To be sure, there were elections and there were even political parties. But only members of the merchant guilds—and that almost meant only those who were successful in trade or business—could vote. It was a middle-class or an upper-middle-class government. Noblemen were excluded from taking part in it. The plain people were left out of it too.

But the Venetian government was neither a tyranny nor a democracy based on merchant guilds. It was an oligarchy.

An oligarchy, according to the dictionary, is a form of government in which power is vested in the few. In the case of Venice, it was vested in the *very* few. But if it was a government *by* the few, it was also a government *for* the many. And that is probably why it endured for so long.

The United States, seemingly so firm and established, is less than two hundred years old; the British Empire—at least that phase of the British Empire when it was an oligarchy governed by its own noble lords—did not last four hundred years. But more or less self-governing Venice stretched out its existence for eleven centuries. Its rule by the oligarchy lasted for eight.

In the beginning, of course, there was no government at all. No government was needed. The Marsh Gauls, when they first came to the islands, were in many ways like the American frontiersmen. Very often clad in hides of the wild deer—or of some other wild animal—and producing all they ate or used, they lived for themselves and by themselves and often at some distance from their nearest neighbor. Their only problem was the wind and weather. What did you do when, as often happened, an unusually high tide flooded the little hummock upon which your hovel stood? How did you get to the wild ducks and the pochard and to the gleaming schools of fish that you either traded or lived

The Doge and People Praying for the Recovery of the Relics of St. Mark.
Thirteenth-century wall mosaic in St. Mark's, Venice.

Gentile Bellini. *Procession of the True Cross in St. Mark's Square.*
Gallerie dell'Academia, Venice.

First overleaf: Canaletto. *Arrival of the Imperial Ambassador at the Ducal Palace.* Aldo Crespi Collection, Milan.

Second overleaf: Andrea Vicentino. *The Battle of Lepanto.* Doge's Palace, Venice.

Giovanni Battista Tiepolo. A carnival scene.
Museo de Arte Moderno, Barcelona.

on, when the channels through the estuaries were frozen tight, as they very often were?

But after the first invasions and the mass emigration to the lagoons, it was another matter. Now there were towns or at least villages instead of isolated shacks, and these towns or villages had to be governed. Somehow or other they found tough, hard-headed officials to do this. These were known as *tribuni maritimi* (tribunes of the salt sea), but no one is quite sure just who they were and how they were chosen. It is thought that at least some of them were descendants of the Roman centurions (a centurion was the Roman equivalent of a top sergeant), who, with their men, were given lands in rural Italy as a reward for their military services. But mixed in with them were refugees of Gothic, Lombard, and even Frankish blood, and certainly there were some Byzantines. (One of the early Venetian chief magistrates was named Galla Gaulo—Galla the Gaul.) Perhaps some of them were elected, but probably most of them were appointed. At first by Rome, and later by Byzantium.

Only one thing is certain. No maritime tribune had any authority outside of his own town or village. The lagoon had no central government, and would not have one for many years to come—not until after the Lombards had driven out the Byzantines and taken over northern Italy.

Then, with no strong protector near at hand, the little Venices decided that in self-defense they must become one big Venice. And with one Venetian ruler.

"In 697," a historian tells us, "the nobles, the clergy, and the citizens" of all the lagoon towns "met at Heracliana and elected a duke." In their soft language, they called him their *doxe* (pronounced *doe-chay*), but we call him—and today everybody calls him—the doge.

He was to be—and he was—an absolute ruler: just as absolute as the Duke of Milan or any other absolute lord on the mainland!

As a matter of fact, his power may have had even fewer limits. At any rate, he tried to make people think so. He put on all the trappings of a Byzantine emperor. He wore a long ermine-trimmed mantle of imperial purple, and like the Byzantine emperor, shoes of brilliant scarlet. (The famous *corno*—the official hooked cap of the doges which you can see in paintings by Titian and others—was not introduced until after 1300.) Over his head was the richly brocaded imperial umbrella. On one occasion, it was presented to the doge by the pope himself.

But there was much more to being a doge than glitter and pomp. His authority was commensurate with the magnificence which surrounded him. After he had been chosen, the new doge was carried in triumph through the city until he reached the Church of St. Mark's. There he was crowned by the *primiciero* (the chief clergyman of the church), who then placed in his hands a bejeweled scepter and the red and gold banner of St. Mark. This done, the doge was allowed to proceed to the ducal palace through a jostling crowd made up of almost every man in Venice. He came out upon a balcony, and was greeted with a mighty shout. It was the people swearing allegiance to him and crying: "Long live our noble duke!"

After that, there were few, if any, who could say nay to him, for his rule extended into every nook and corner. He presided over the high court of justice. (The court was the administrative center of the city. It did not limit itself to matters of law.) He appointed all the officials and all the judges. He was commander-in-chief of the army and navy. He was the only man who could sign treaties. He was the only man who could declare war or make peace. Finally, the treasury of Venice was so completely in his hands that it was almost impossible to tell which funds belonged to the state and which were the doge's private property.

To be sure, the doge did have to be elected by a popular assembly of all the people, but most doges found a way of making this assembly do what they wanted. For one thing, the doges were the only ones who could convene it. For another, most doges saw to it that their successors were named while they were still living—usually a son or at least a relative.

Except for a very short period (726–742) when the doge was replaced by a master of the soldiers, this rule by doges who had absolute power lasted for three hundred and thirty-five years. It was an important period, for it was then that the Venetians moved out from the lagoon onto the high seas. It was under these early doges that Venice first started her march toward prosperity and power, that she first became not only a city but a great state.

But if Venice did prosper abroad—and in the market place—not everything went smoothly, and particularly at home. Ambitious men have always found power worth fighting for, and there were plenty of ambitious men in Venice. Above all, there were three ambitious families—the Partecipazii, the Candiani, and the Orseoli—and each one of them wanted to make the office of doge its personal property. At one time or another, each of them almost succeeded.

There were eighteen doges between 811, when Angelo Partecipazio ascended the ducal throne—and moved the seat of government to Rivo Alto—and 1026, when the last Orseolo ended his reign, and of these, seven were Partecipazii, five Candiani, and three Orseoli. Only three doges did not belong to any of the three families.

It is easy to see what was happening. Each of the three families was striving to make the office of doge hereditary—and then to seize it. They wanted a Partecipazio (or a Candiano or an Orseolo) Duke of Venice, just as there was a Visconti Duke of Milan.

But fortunately a new class of people was growing up in Venice—the class of wealthy aristocrats—and they were distressed at the disorders this struggle for power brought about, and alarmed at the fact that hardly a doge had died peacefully in office. It damaged their reputation and hurt their trade. Moreover, they had an instrument to act with. These merchant aristocrats—and some members of the lower classes—had slowly evolved a council to take care of mercantile matters. In a way, it was a Chamber of Commerce, but it could act politically too. In due time, it did.

It had to, for ducal arrogance had grown by leaps and bounds, and in 976, Pietro Candiano IV had not only dared to marry the niece of the Holy Roman emperor, Otto, and to act like an emperor himself, but while civil chief of state, he had appointed his son patriarch of Grado, or religious head.

Not even the fact that riots broke out as a result—riots in which the angry Venetians burned the Doge's Palace, the churches of St. Mark and St. Theodore, and three hundred private houses, and murdered the doge and a baby son—changed the situation. Pietro's successors—among them another Candiano and three Orseoli—were equally high-handed.

The doges must be curbed, and the council set out to do this.

In 1032, it passed a drastic law. From thenceforward no doge could name a coruler, whether his son or anyone else. At the same time the council gave the doge two personal councilors. They were supposed to give him advice, but actually they were watchdogs. It was their job to keep him from doing anything the merchant noblemen might not like.

To be sure, the people still elected the doge, and sometimes they did it in the noisiest possible way. In 1071, for example, the bishop and his clergy went to the Lido to celebrate a mass for the soul of the late doge, Domenico Contarini. A huge crowd followed them in every kind of vessel. When the services ended, some of the crowd surged ashore and surrounded a nobleman, Domenico Selvo.

"We want him for doge!" they roared. "We praise him and elect him!"

Then they took him back to the city, where the provisional government was obliged to ratify this popular choice.

Doge Selvo did not remain popular for long, but that was largely on account of his wife. She was a Byzantine princess and she shocked the still somewhat provincial Venetians with her Byzantine ways. "Why, her room reeks with perfume," they whispered, "and every day she not only washes her hands but her whole body! She washes either with scented water or with dew collected by her slaves. And she does not even touch her food with her fingers. Instead, she has it lifted to her mouth with a strange three-pronged instrument."

But although the people whispered about their dogaressa, they still clung to the privilege of choosing their doge.

Until 1172, that is. In that year, the whole city rose in anger against Doge Vitale Michiele because his incompetence had caused a Venetian fleet to fall into the hands of the Byzantines. He was bloodily assassinated. Then, when it came to choosing a new doge, the people handed over their power to the council, which now included every important person in the city and was called the Great Council.

In theory, to be sure, the people still had to ratify the Great Council's choice. "This is Messer Your Doge *if it please you!*" they were told when the new doge was presented to them.

But they always *were* pleased. They *had* to be, for it was the Great Council—and the other governing bodies created by it—which had the real power. And this power grew and grew until finally, in 1297, the council took a step which the doges had not ever been able to take. It passed a law by which it made itself hereditary. This was the so-called *Serrata del Consiglio,* or locking up of the council.

In the early days, at least theoretically, anybody in Venice could be elected to this body—a citizen or even a workingman just as much as a noble. But in practice, only a few members were from the two lower classes; a majority of its members were noblemen. For instance, in 1261 twenty Contarini, nineteen Querini, nineteen Dandoli, fifteen Morosini, twelve Michieli, eleven Falieri, eight or nine Tiepoli, eight or nine Foscari—and of course representatives of many other noble families too—sat in a council of two hundred and forty-two. The exact number is not known, but the noblemen were in control, and they wanted to make sure that they remained in control.

So they locked the council up. After eleven years of argument they enacted a provision which closed the council doors to newcomers. In its first form, it provided that only those men (and their heirs) who had sat on the council between 1293 and 1297 were thenceforth eligible to serve on it, and even they had to be approved by twelve votes in a screening committee of forty.

Later, however, the eligibility rules were broadened a little. A special committee of three electors had the power to submit any name it wished, and anyone who had an ancestor who had served on the council between 1172 and 1293 was also eligible. So too were members of the twelve families who, according to legend, had elected the first doge.

The name of everyone who was eligible to serve on the Great Council was inscribed in large black letters in an official register which has gone down in history as the Golden Book. It was a richly bound book—that is what gave it its name—but it was not a fat one, for only two hundred families ever found a place in it. Two hundred families in almost seven hundred years!

But the Great Council was not the only governing body in Venice. It could not be, for despite all its restrictions it soon grew too big and unwieldy. At one time the Great Council had sixteen hundred and twelve persons sitting on it. Moreover, it met only on Sundays. For, remember, the noblemen who served on it were practicing merchants too, and on weekdays they went to their warehouses and their wharves.

Consequently—and very early—a second body, the Pregadi (invited ones), or Senate, was created. Originally it had only sixty members, and these had to be at least forty years old and were elected by the Great Council from its own number. In a way, it was the executive committee of the Great Council. "It is the soul of the Republic!" cried an enthusiastic senator and he was quite right.

Unlike the Great Council, the Senate met every day. (Presumably when a merchant nobleman reached forty he could spare more time from his business!)

But the Senate too grew and grew until finally it had three hundred members. Clearly it needed a smaller executive body which could at least prepare its business for it. Very promptly it created one.

This was the Collegio (College), and it numbered twenty-six—the ten members of the Signory (the doge and his closest advisers) and sixteen *savii* (special councilors). The latter were elected by the Senate for a term of six months, and three of them acted as department heads. One *savio* was the Secretary of Defense (Secretary of the Army and Navy); a second did the duties of the Secretary of the Treasury; the third acted as Minister of Munitions and Supply.

Besides the above, there was one other governmental institution of importance. This was the famous Dieci, or Council of Ten.

In some ways it was the most important of all. For if one can believe all the tales—and tall tales—that were told about it, there was not a Venetian, high or low, who did not live in deadly fear of its activities. From the days when it was first set up until the time when the adventurer and scoundrel Casanova fell into its hands in 1755, there was no end to the hair-raising stories about its doings, and especially the doings of its agents, the sinister *signori di notti* (night patrolmen), who supposedly lurked in every dark corner and muffled their victims' heads in their cloaks before whisking them off to vanish and never more be seen.

Even the motto of the Dieci was terrifying: *Secretum et iterum secretum*—secrecy and yet more secrecy. However, it was much more than an intelligence agency, or even a secret police such as those set up in modern times by Communist and Fascist states. It could exercise surveillance and it did. It took people into temporary or even permanent custody. It could also hear cases and try them, and when it did, it was judge and jury all in one.

Yet the Dieci came into being to fill a real need. During the fifty-eight years which followed the locking-up of the Great Council, there was a whole series of conspiracies whose aim was to overthrow the government by oligarchy and set up a one-man tyranny. Three of them were very serious.

In 1300, Marino Bocconio, a wealthy middle-class merchant who was seething because he was excluded from all part in the government, called on the people to rise in defense of their rights, and with ten followers, marched on the ducal palace. But the people did not rise and Marino and his men were seized. They were hanged head downward where all Venice could see them.

In 1310, it was an aristocrat who led the uprising. Biamonte Tiepolo was a member of one of the oldest families in Venice, but like many an aristocrat before and after, he sided with the people—the plain Venetians called him "the great knight errant" because of his dashing ways—and in particular, he opposed the closing of the council. He wanted the people to rule the city. He thought he could rule the people.

On June 15, he and his fellow conspirators—among them were other noblemen, including a Badoer and a Querini—took to the streets. "Liberty!" they shouted. "Liberty! Liberty!"

But the doge had been warned, and he sent soldiers against them. They were swiftly routed, and Badoer was executed. Tiepolo, the great knight errant, managed somehow to escape. But he was condemned to exile, and he lived in exile, still hoping and plotting, for the next twenty years.

Finally, in 1355, came the third conspiracy, and it was the most serious of all, for the doge himself was the chief conspirator. He was Marino Faliero. (The English poet Lord Byron wrote a blank-verse play about him.)

There are many stories about how this conspiracy came about and why a doge should have plotted against his own government. A favorite one is that Marino's wife had been insulted by a young aristocrat, Michel Steno, and that when Steno was only lightly punished, her husband burned for revenge. Others say that Venice was doing badly in a war with Genoa, and that Marino felt that a dictator was needed.

Whatever the reason, plot and scheme the doge did, and so well were his plans laid that if one of the conspirators had not gone to a friend and warned him to stay in his house if he did not wish to be killed, it might have succeeded. The friend told the story to a councilor he knew, and the councilor informed the council. Marino was swiftly arrested and he confessed. He and his colleagues were condemned to death.

They were executed without delay; the lesser leaders were hanged, and Marino was beheaded on the very spot where he had been proclaimed doge only a year before. "Death—terrible death—has come to the traitor!" cried the executioner.

And where Marino's portrait should have been hung with those of the other doges in the Doge's Palace, there was hung instead a panel painted black. *This*, read a legend on it, *is the place reserved for Marino Faliero, who was decapitated for his crimes.*

Although none of these conspiracies succeeded, the first two so frightened the ruling nobility that, in order to deal with any future ones, they set up a special body. This was the Dieci. At first it was a temporary body, but in 1335 it was made permanent. It was then that it got its name.

Actually, its powers were never as great as the people imagined, and much care was taken to make sure that no group or faction could ever control it. Its members were elected for a term of only three months, and no one could be re-elected until a year had passed. Furthermore, only one member of any family could serve on it at a time, and anyone haled before it was at least supposed to have the right to appeal and to be represented by a lawyer. Finally, the doge and his council always sat with the Ten. This was to protect those who came before them.

Nevertheless, the Council of Ten had power enough to do its business. No one was exempt from its jurisdiction, not even the doge. Indeed, it was the Ten which sentenced Marino Faliero. And although it did hold public hearings, its deliberations took place behind closed doors, and it did not have to turn over information that came to it to anyone, not even to the Senate or to the Signory.

Most of the judgments passed by the Ten were based on things told them by spies or informers. A man's brother— or his son or his wife—might report political activity plotted in the privacy of his own home, or even criticism of the government uttered there. An enemy need only toss an unsigned accusation into the Bocca di Leone (the open mouth of a lion whose statue stood near the Doge's Palace). Soon there would be a knock at the door of the man accused, and before he knew it he would be facing grim judges in a dimly lighted chamber. If he was not lucky he might shortly find himself in the Piombi (the Leads) or the Pozzi (the Cisterns). The Piombi were cells under the lead roof of the Doge's Palace and a prisoner scorched and suffered there. The Pozzi were dank prisons beneath the canal where he shivered as water dripped from the walls.

It was the Council of Ten—or rather, fear of the Council of Ten—that kept the other governing bodies in power, and it was these other governing bodies that ruled Venice. The doge had become merely a figurehead.

To be sure, he was an expensive figurehead, for not only was the greater part of his expenses paid for by the state, but he was given an annual salary of fifteen thousand ducats.

It took Andrea Barbarigo eighteen years of active business to accumulate the same amount!

But although there were strong doges such as Enrico Dandolo, or Francesco Foscari, or Andrea Gritti, who led the Venetians back to greatness after the battle of Agnadello, most doges were like the kings and queens in a constitutional monarchy. They reigned—that is, they sat upon the throne —but they did not rule.

A man could not even intrigue to get himself elected doge, for most doges were chosen by a complicated procedure which made being elected almost like winning the grand prize in a lottery.

Here is how it was done in 1268, and it was almost certainly done the same way in other years. When the old doge died, the ducal councilors convened the Great Council in St. Mark's, and each member drew a wax ball from a gilded box held by a handsome youth. Inside of thirty of them was a piece of parchment with the word *lector* written on it. The ones who drew these balls were called electors.

These thirty repeated the performance, except that this time only nine pellets had the word *lector* on it, and the nine thus chosen chose forty electors. The forty chose twelve— this time the balls were drawn from a hat—and these twelve chose twenty-five. These twenty-five chose another nine, and the nine another forty. This final forty chose eleven and the final eleven chose forty-one. The forty-one chose the doge. The first candidate to receive twenty-five of their votes was elected doge.

Thereupon, he was taken to St. Mark's, where he signed the *promissio*, or promise. This was the equivalent of our modern oath of office. It was a written list of the things that the doge could do and the things he could not do. In one case it was nine pages long.

But what the doge could do was very little. He could appoint the patriarch, and he could appoint the clergy of St. Mark's, and he could lay propositions before the Great Council. But he could not make them vote upon these or even discuss them. He presided over that august body and over the Senate and the College, but he could not speak in any of them.

(Two doges did defy this law. Michel Steno—he was the one who as a youth had insulted Marino Faliero's wife—roared his defiance at the Senate. "I will speak and I dare you to punish me!" he cried. Tomaso Mocenigo cheerfully paid a fine of a thousand ducats rather than not move that the Doge's Palace, which had been burned, immediately be rebuilt.)

Although he was head of the government and was addressed as Monsignor the Doge, and Most Serene Prince, and although all Venetian money was issued in his name and stamped with his image, the doge could not receive foreign ambassadors or open messages from foreign potentates except in the presence of his advisers.

The Venetians saw to it, too, that their doges lived up to all this. As soon as a doge was named, three special officials were appointed. They were called correctors, and they were no longer the unofficial watchdogs of an earlier day. "It is your duty," they were instructed, "to keep a close eye upon the doge and to see to it that he is the chief of state of the Republic—the chief of state, and not its master." Nor did this very careful scrutiny end even after the doge had died. His whole conduct—but especially his financial conduct—was thoroughly examined, and if he had done anything wrong, and particularly if he had misused state funds, his heirs had to make good.

No such limitations applied to the oligarchy—the few

who now ruled Venice and who ruled it to the end of its days.
The Great Council—and the Senate and the College, which
were really committees of the Great Council—governed
without any interference, and in the way they thought best.

Obviously, since the council's members were now all
merchant noblemen and had been since the closing of the
council, the way the government thought best was the one
that did the most good for the foreign commerce on which
they all depended.

"All the merchant nobles of Venice," Professor Lane tells
us, "operated as one large company of which the Senate was
the Board of Directors."

Almost all did. There were a few who looked out for their
own interests first. Said a writer on Venice: "Members of
the Senate were also merchants and sometimes voted in
favor of their own mercantile interests. Those with plenty
of spices on hand were known to vote against sending galleys to bring more spices. Shipowners wanted freight rates
fixed relatively high."

But more were like Doge Andrea Contarini. In 1377 the
Venetians had been defeated at sea during a war with
Genoa, and a great Genoese fleet was at their doorstep. The
Venetian treasury was almost empty. Things looked black
indeed.

The doge did not hesitate. "Sell everything I own and
lend the proceeds to Venice," he told his agents. "If Genoa
conquers, what difference does it make what happens to my
investments!"

Even more remarkable, the merchant noblemen of Venice
realized something that some people are only beginning
to realize today, and that is that if there are a few who are
very rich and many living in abject poverty, the riches of
the wealthy are in danger too. For that reason, while they

encouraged the accumulation of wealth, they saw to it that there was as little poverty as possible by providing carefully, and by law, for every need.

We have already seen, for example, what the oligarch government did to assure the safety, well-being, and even comfort of sailors and shipmen; but the government also took care—perhaps even better care—of the Venetians who remained behind.

Except possibly fish, waterfowl, fruit, and vegetables, which came from the lagoon and its islands, everything that was used in Venice had to be imported. The meat which they ate boiled or roasted. The grain which they baked into bread. The wine they quaffed so gustily. Stone and marble for their buildings, and wood to make their ships. Raw materials for their lace, glass, wool, silk, and gilt-leather industries, which now ran a close second to their overseas trade, and which by the fifteenth and sixteenth centuries supported many thousands. The government saw to it that they were imported.

Equally important, the Venetian government saw to it that the Venetians—every single Venetian—had the money with which to buy these things. And that they got it through work, not charity.

This the Venetian government did by strictly supervising private enterprise (even the private enterprise of the oligarchs) with an eye to what was best for one and all. For example, when jobs were scarce, hours of work were regulated so that everybody could find some employment. But wages were controlled also, so that, whenever possible, no employer had to pay so much that he could not make a profit, and no employee received so little that he could not live. Even the elderly were taken care of—they too were given work and not alms.

A 1443 law provided that certain kinds of foodstuffs could be sold only by those who "because of their age could go to sea no more," and who could no longer perform any other kind of strenuous labor. The law was passed "so they could take care of their own declining years and those of their poor families."

This does not mean that there were no beggars in Venice. A 1582 census showed that there were one hundred and eighty-seven. But this was after Venice had begun to decline, and there were few indeed compared to the thousands in the other cities of Italy, where hordes of blind, halt and sore-infested beggars were a familiar sight. The Venetian government did not approve of beggars and saw to it that few needed to beg.

Venice in Her Days of Splendor

It was Venice's firm and solid government—and the stability and security which it brought—that gave the Venetians the opportunity to make their city into the Venice which Martino da Canale described in 1267, and the even more dazzling one which Philippe de Commines looked upon in 1495 and Henry III of France visited some eighty years later.

They used this opportunity to the fullest, for although they worshiped wealth, the Venetians also loved the good things of the world, and they could see no point in passing them up by hoarding all or even much of the money they had amassed. What good, they said, would the riches of the Indies do them if they were locked up in strongboxes? Better to spend it lavishly and then gain more.

Spend it they did.

They spent it, for example, to build some of the most magnificent public edifices that the world has ever seen, as well as the most luxurious and splendid private homes.

In 1561, Francesco Sansovino, son of the famous sculptor Jacopo Sansovino, wrote one of the first guide books ever to be published. He called it *Notable Things in the City of Venice,* and in it he described these homes.

"There is not a town in Europe which has more and larger palaces than this town of Venice. In the other towns of Italy, for example"—in Naples, Milan, Genoa, Florence, Bologna, and even Rome—"you will not find more than three or four buildings worthy of the name 'palace,' but in Venice you can count them by the hundreds." Indeed, they were so plentiful that the Venetians did not even call them by this name. "Out of modesty, we call them houses," said Francesco. "We save the name 'palace' for the Doge's Palace."

The Venetians also spent their money to dress like birds of paradise or peacocks—the men as well as the women.

"The ladies of Venice are exquisitely beautiful," wrote Marino Sanudo during the fifteenth century. "And they are always adorned with jewels." He then gave some of the details. When a great foreign lady came to Venice, a hundred and thirty of the noblest Venetian ladies met her. They were clad in garments of silk and *colendena*—another rich, rare cloth—and these garments were always worth at least a hundred ducats, and sometimes they were worth three hundred. "On their fingers they wore rings set with balas rubies, sapphires, emeralds, and pearls. A woman thought herself poor if hers were not worth five hundred ducats!"

Another observer told almost the same story: "People who know what they are talking about and who tell the truth," he said, "informed me that when the pope's nephew visited Venice the clothes worn by the women who greeted him were worth three hundred thousand gold pieces." He was probably not talking of ducats, but of smaller gold coins. Even so, it was a lot of money!

It was not only on clothes that the Venetian ladies spent extravagant amounts. The way they did their hair is legendary, and as you can see in paintings by almost every Venetian artist, some of the hair styles were as fantastic as hair styles can be today. It was always blond hair too, although the Venetians, like other Italians, are naturally a dark-haired people. It was blond because the Venetian ladies wanted to be blond and so made themselves blond. They daubed their hair with all kinds of strange concoctions, and then sat upon their *altane* (rooftop balconies) and let the sun bleach it.

The Venetian ladies also spent much money on their complexions. Gone were the days when they had jeered at Doge Selvo's wife for her luxurious Byzantine ways. They themselves now used all kinds of unguents to keep their skin smooth and fair, and one Venetian beauty wanted so badly to preserve the delicate pink of her cheeks that she slept with a piece of raw veal soaked in milk pressed upon them. They also drenched themselves with perfume, and poured into their baths scents based on musk, ambergris, essence of aloes, leaves of the citron tree, lavender, and even mint.

Then they put on a rose-colored or a sea-blue garment and slipped their feet into *zoccoli*. *Zoccoli* were Venetian slippers with heels more than eighteen inches high. In the beginning, these heels were lower than that and were designed to keep the wearer's feet from the mud. But they grew taller and taller as one lady tried to outdo the other, until finally they became so exaggerated that a famous beauty fell and injured herself. After that it became the custom for promenading ladies to walk only with the help of a slave.

The men's costumes were equally gorgeous. In the days of old, at least the aristocrats, both young and old, had worn long stately robes and somber velvet hats. But as the city grew richer and richer, these were more and more often put aside to be used only on state occasions or when the Great Council met (there were even cabinets in the Doge's Palace in which to store them until they were needed). Instead the men broke out in green and blue and scarlet finery, and their fingers flaunted almost as many rings as did the women's. And no Venetian felt that he was really important unless he wore a heavy golden chain about his neck.

At least some efforts were made to control the men's extravagance, however. More than one youth was sent back to his home for overdressing, and on one occasion Doge Cristòforo Moro (1462–1471) was urged by the council to issue an edict forbidding young men to wear long hair, "because it makes them look like women."

During the days of their grandeur, the Venetians also gave banquets such as had not been seen since the days of the Romans. Some of the banquets for visiting potentates lasted for six hours, and Venetian festivals were so colorful and exciting that the streets and piazzas were filled with people from all over the world.

For a good part of the year, these festivals were almost continuous.

First came Christmas. At this time of the year, gifts were exchanged by one and all, but particularly by the fowlers, who came in from the lagoons as they had done ever since there was a Venice. Their boats were laden with the birds they had snared—among them "some of those shore birds which the French call mallards." They presented two thousand of these to the doge and his noblemen. They also presented "more than a thousand capons" to the more important of the citizens.

Then came the Carnival, which began immediately after Christmas and lasted until Ash Wednesday. The next festival was Easter, which followed the bleak forty days of Lent and the raw, cold winter weather which brought fog and sometimes even snow.

At Easter, the twenty-two chaplains of St. Mark's put on pluvials (long churchly garments) made of cloth of gold, and ceremoniously conducted the doge to their church, where High Mass in honor of the Resurrection was joyously celebrated.

Other Venetian festivals—some of the other Venetian festivals—were Ascension (when the sea was married); *Corpus Domini* (then velvet-clad noblemen and clergy robed in white carried heavy wax candles through the city as they do in Bellini's painting in the gallery of the Academia in Venice); the feast of the Redeemer (on this occasion a bridge of boats was stretched to the Giudecca); and two festivals in honor of St. Mark, one in January and the other in October.

Besides these, there was the festival of the *Marie* in honor of the captured brides. At that time the doge—with his state umbrella held over his head and the principal prelates in embroidered vestments—led a stately procession of six highly decorated boats through the city. On board were twelve maidens, all of them crowned with gold, whose dowries the state paid every year as a thank offering for the brides' rescue. This festival took place on February 2, and hence usually coincided with the Carnival. Finally there was the so-called Labors of Hercules, which was a rough-and-tumble battle between two factions of the people—the Castellani, mainly shipyard workers, who lived in the eastern part of Venice, and the Niccolotti, for the most part fishermen, who lived in the western part. This was a noisy affair of shouting, fisticuffs, and the banging of quarterstaves, and at the end the losers were tossed into the canal to the delight of the winners and all those who did not belong to either faction.

There were also numerous regattas—even one for women —which began at the eastern tip of the city and often ran the whole length of the Grand Canal. And on special occasions, receptions were held for state visitors.

Of all these festivals, the Carnival was the favorite, for it was a never-ending day-long, night-long kaleidoscope of color and sound, and nothing drab or sobersided was allowed a part in it. Everywhere there was jostling and bustling, and the tintinnabulation of bells and the honking of cheap horns.

The Malmseys—the name given to the shops where Malmsey, a popular sweet wine that came from Monemvasia in Greece, was sold—thronged with old friends and new friends. Along the quaysides and in front of the Doge's Palace, acrobats and tightrope walkers performed for such coins as the onlookers would toss to them.

Astrologers with peaked caps and star-spangled robes set up their booths in every piazza and, for a small sum, told the fortune of anyone who came to them. On the piazzas there were puppet shows—they were not very different from our Punch and Judy shows, for Punch came from the Italian Polichinella—and all about, there were strolling musicians and portable menageries and cosmoramas (the latter pictured scenes made to seem real by lights and mirrors).

Finally, on Shrove Tuesday, or Mardi Gras, came the climax. Ever since 1162, when the Venetians had defeated a rebellious patriarch of Grado, the citizens of that city had been obliged to send Venice a bull and twelve fat hogs each year, and on Shrove Tuesday these were released in the Piazza to be hunted down by the crowd and then publicly butchered by their captors. Later, organized bullfights were added. And at night there was a display of fireworks.

Even babes in arms were taken to the Carnival. But that was probably so their nurses could go too.

The Venetians also spent their money on making certain that the cupboard was never bare.

Francesco Sansovino tells what a task this was. In his guide book, he says that the Venetians had to buy five hundred oxen, two hundred and fifty calves, and "an unbelievable amount of goats and poultry" every week just to take care of what they ate day in and day out. All these had to be transported from the mainland on heavy barges.

But the Venetians did not limit themselves to such plain fare. A diarist of the day says that they ate "partridges, pheasants, peacocks, doves, and every other kind of bird you could imagine." A shopping list shows that they bought wild chicken, turkeys, grouse, sturgeon, and olive oil. They knew about caviar, truffles, "pear-shaped lemons," and every kind of salad.

They also brought in Bologna sausages, Modena sausages, pig's brains, country cheese, pasta from Genoa, thrushes, geese, quail, and such vegetables and fruits as almonds, cherries, squash, muscatel pears, apricots, melons, plums, grapes, and peaches. They had not one but two markets for seafood—and in these one could buy almost anything that lived in the water or swam, from lobsters to every kind of silvery fish.

The men of Venice took equal pains to quench their thirst. A wine list of the day gives proof of this. Besides Malmsey, it includes Burgundy, Graves, Rhine wine, Moselle, and muscatel, all from France and Germany, as well as canary, the vintages of Austria, Hungary, Cyprus, and Greece, and red and white table wines from nearby northern Italy.

Of course, not everybody in Venice could afford all these good things to eat and drink. At least some of them were for the rich only. But just as it had regulated wages and hours, the Venetian government tried to make certain that no one was unable to afford anything he really needed. In part, it did this by fixing prices. In the early 1500s, for example, beef could not be sold for more than two *soldi* a pound and olive oil for more than four *soldi*. (A *soldo* was the Venetian shilling.) There were officers called *carrizadori del comune* (municipal inspectors) to see to it that the law was enforced.

But even as the Venetians spent all this fortune on living well—on food and drink and lavish festivities—they did not entirely forget that there were other things. They wanted their city to be the most glorious in the world as well as the richest, and like many rich men before and after them, they realized that culture and art—writing and philosophy and painting and sculpture—were among the things that would win them this glory. They realized, too, that these were something that they could buy, and they set out to buy them.

They were not always completely successful. For instance, during the days of its greatness and grandeur, Venice did not produce a single truly great writer. But it did shelter many a lesser one. Indeed, not until London in the days of Queen Elizabeth I, when some of the greatest playwrights in the world lived by writing penny-dreadful potboilers, was there ever such a hack-writer's paradise. There were translators from almost every language in the world; authors of pamphlets and treatises on any subject that could be dreamed up; journalists who made a living by threatening to write libels if they were not paid to write praise; and poets whose epics—or even sonnets—saw the light of day only because some important man sponsored them. These shabby men, for all but a few were down at the heels, never stopped quarreling with one another, and since many of them were as skillful with their daggers as with their pens, they kept the city in a constant turmoil. But they made life in Venice very exciting.

Most of these writers were not Venetians. They were Italians from every other part of Italy, and they came to Venice for one reason only: Venice proclaimed herself the home of free speech. Compared to other places in that day and age, she really was. A man could say anything he wanted to in Venice—that is, if he did not attack the city or its government. He could call the pope a rogue and hurl insults at every king and duke and marquis in the whole world. As long as he praised the doge, he was safe.

Venice had more success as a refuge for scholarship and learning.

In a way, this was almost an accident. The merchants of Venice were not any more interested in ancient Greek poetry and philosophy than businessmen anywhere else might have been, but they knew a good thing when they saw it; and beginning in the second half of the fourteenth century, they thought they saw a good thing. For it was at that time that the Turks began to move into Europe; and when they did, the scholars and the men of learning who were scattered all over the Byzantine Empire began to wonder if this was any longer the place for them. Particularly now that Italy welcomed them—Italy, whose own scholars had been taught by Boccaccio and Petrarch that a man could not call himself really cultured unless he was able to read Greek.

They came to Venice first, and this was natural. Venice was a city where almost every language was spoken: not only the native Venetian dialect, but Spanish, French, Italian, Provençal—*and* Greek! There was a large Greek colony in Venice. Venice and Constantinople had been doing business with each other for almost a thousand years.

With them, the scholars brought their precious manuscripts—the manuscripts that had been a source of glory to ancient Greece. Homer and Plato and even Aesop. These they smuggled to Venice in leaky, storm-tossed vessels.

The Venetians tried to persuade the scholars to stay, and sometimes they succeeded. Not always, however, or even often, for the Medici of Florence usually bid higher for their services. But on at least one occasion, the Venetians made so good an impression that they won for their city a treasure which Venice still has.

It came to them from Cardinal Bessarion, who was perhaps the greatest of all fifteenth-century Greek scholars. Cardinal Bessarion was a diplomat too, and he traveled widely trying to persuade the Christian princes to march against the Turk. But his scholarship came first. Indeed, it is said that he would have been elected pope if he had not refused to interrupt his studies when a committee of cardinals came to offer him the office.

During his travels Bessarion had accumulated a large collection of Greek and Latin manuscripts—he himself had translated books by some of the greatest Greek writers. When he died in Ravenna in 1472, he left them all to Venice as an expression of his gratitude for what Venice had done for him and men like him. These manuscripts now form the most important part of the Marciana Library, which is still one of the finest in Italy.

In the days of her grandeur and glory, Venice made another, and even more important, contribution to culture. She became the world center of fine printing.

It is said that the art of making books from movable type

was invented in China by a man named Pi Cheng during the years between 1058 and 1061. It was reinvented in Europe four hundred years later—either by the world-famous German printer Gutenberg or by a Dutchman named Coster. But it was the Germans who really developed it, and it was two Germans, Johann and Wendelin de Spira, who brought it to Venice in 1469. Printing flourished in Venice as nowhere before, and there were several reasons for this.

In the first place, Venice had the manuscripts. And, in the men seeking to earn their living by the pen, Venice had those eager to edit these manuscripts. She also had many skilled artisans, men who could be trained as printers. Perhaps even more important, Venice was the greatest market in the world. Printing became profitable because it could turn a codex which only the rich could afford into a book which almost anyone who could read could buy. And Venice was thronged with possible buyers. Venice also had the cheapest and finest paper in the world. And finally, she had the capital to support this new venture.

But not even printing—although at his sign of the anchor and dolphin, Aldus Manutius (1450–1515) probably printed more beautiful books than anyone before or since—was Venice's greatest contribution to the world of culture.

Unquestionably her greatest contribution was Venetian painting, and this more than any of the other arts was made possible by the munificence of the Venetian noblemen, who loved painting far more than they did either letters or learning. They saw to it that every Venetian artist who was worth anything—and some who were not—was given one well-paying commission after another. No artist starved in Venice. Many of them became as wealthy as the rich men they painted for.

Here are some of Venice's greatest artists.

Paolo Veneziano and his sons, Luca and Giovanni. The three Bellini—Jacopo and his sons, Giovanni and Gentile. Giorgio di Castelfranco, who is better known by his nickname, Giorgione (Big George). He died when he was thirty-two and might have been the greatest of them all had he lived longer. Titian—he *was* the greatest. Tintoretto, another nickname, meaning "the little dyer"; his real name was Jacopo Robusti. Veronese. And Jacopo Bassano.

It is not possible here to tell the whole story of the wonderful paintings these men did. They were to be found everywhere in Venice and in many other places too: on the façade of the German warehouse; in private houses; in most of the churches; and on the walls of the great chambers in public buildings. The men who did them were honored by their fellow Venetians. Several of them were renowned throughout the world.

Gentile Bellini, for example, painted the portraits of two doges and many other prominent Venetians, and when the Turkish sultan, Mohammed II, heard of these, he sent for the artist. Mohammed wanted his portrait done too, and when it was finished, he was so pleased with it that he made Gentile a *bey*. This was akin to knighting him. The sultan also asked the painter to build a bridge across the Golden Horn, but Gentile declined. He wanted to return to Venice.

Titian went to Augsburg in Austria to paint the emperor Charles V, and to Rome to paint Pope Paul III. There was hardly a duke or marquis in Italy who did not want to have one of his works. This was true of most of the other Venetian artists. Their paintings were in demand from England and France to Spain and Naples.

Regardless of their origin, all these artists were, and lived like, great gentlemen. Titian, who lived to be ninety-nine, was perhaps the wealthiest of them. In addition to his house, which was far from modest, he had a garden facing Murano, and there on summer evenings he entertained writers, philosophers, wealthy magnates, highborn princes, and the lovely ladies for whom Venice was famous. Very few of the other Venetian artists lived much less lavishly.

These artists were also fearless and independent. Tintoretto once strode into the apartments of a client who had said he painted far too hastily. A pistol was in his hand.

"What are you going to do?" the client asked him, quaking.

"Take your measure!" said Tintoretto, who then proceeded to measure him in pistol lengths. "Now I will paint your picture," he said when he had finished.

An officer of the Inquisition once rebuked Veronese for painting religious scenes as if they were Venetian banquets. "You paint 'The Marriage at Cana' and 'The Feast in the House of Levi,' and in these scenes, supposedly laid in humble homes in Galilee, you put men in costly garments and women wearing glittering jewels. Instead of honoring Christ, you paint a little monkey playing. This is sacrilegious!"

"I am an artist, not a monk!" Veronese replied.

But even if Venetian artists lived like lords and had the arrogance to match, their brushes were never idle, and the paintings they did, have few if any superiors in the long history of art. Their works are still noted for their warmth, their richness, and their color. Some say that Venetian painters were able to bring these qualities to their painting because they began to use oil very early. Oil painting was developed in Flanders by two brothers, Hubert and Jan Van Eyck, but the Venetians soon took it over and made it their own. The use of oil brought their paintings to glowing life—something that was difficult to achieve in fresco.

The city of Venice was, however, much more than the sum of all its parts. It was much more than the oil paintings that decorated every palace and church. It was more than the books printed by Aldus Manutius and others; and the festivals; and the gatherings of learned men; and the busy hum of the Rialto. It was more than the numerous buildings that made it like an unbelievable stage setting.

Venice itself was much more than all these put together.

"For floor, she has the sea," cried a visitor, "for ceiling, the stars, and for city walls, she has the tides!"

"She astonishes the whole world!" cried another. "In fact, even her name tells of the longing all have to come back to her. Venetia comes from *veni etiam*—this means come back again."

The center of this marvelous city is, and has always been, the great open space which is called the Piazza di San Marco, or just the Piazza. We call it St. Mark's Square.

In the days of Venetian grandeur, there was nothing in the world to compare with it except the Mesé, or Midway— the busy principal street of old Byzantium. Yet for all that, the Piazza occupies only a small part of a city which, as far as area is concerned, is not very large.

Venice is made up of one hundred and seventeen islands intersected by more than a hundred and fifty canals crossed by four hundred bridges, yet its total area is not more than sixteen hundred acres. St. Mark's Square does not cover more than four.

"It is a bowshot long," said an ancient chronicler. Actually, it is about two hundred yards long, and its width is sixty yards at one end, and eighty-four at the other. It is about the size of two football fields.

Even so, the Piazza was the center of most of the city's

activities. To be sure, business—merchant business, that is, or foreign trade—was for the most part conducted on the Rialto, halfway across the city. There, near a huge *mappa-mondo* (map of the world) on which were painted all the Venetian trade routes, everyone who used those trade routes gathered. But everything else happened on or near the Piazza.

It was in the Piazza that Gian Manenti, the master gambler, walked up and down hawking tickets to his lottery—and everyone from great lady to parish priest to humble gardener sought to buy one. It was here that painters—those painters who were not yet well known—tried to sell their paintings. It was here that poets and hack writers read their poems and satires—or got mountebanks or street singers to read them for them.

It was here too—but only in earlier times—that the Venetian could buy (and usually did) anything from trinkets to fish, for until 1504, when they were torn down, the square was filled with hovels and shops.

Finally, it was in St. Mark's Square, or not far off, that every Venetian ceremony or celebration either began or ended. This included the most important ceremony of all, the procession in honor of a new doge.

This procession did not take place every year, of course, for the average length of a doge's reign was between nine and ten years.

It was a popular ceremony and it was in the charge of the Venetian guilds (or *mariegole* as they were called), who supervised every detail of it.

First came the men from the other Venetian cities, such as Torcello and Murano. Those from Murano by tradition brought gondola after gondola filled with cackling fowls which they presented to the new dogaressa. She was allowed to accept them, although she could not accept gifts from foreign princes.

After these came the guildsmen themselves, all gorgeously attired. The master tanners were clad in mantles trimmed with vair and ermine. The secondhand-fur dealers dressed in samite and taffeta. The master tailors wore white cloaks trimmed with vermilion stars. The master vest- and shirt-makers also had capes of white, but theirs were trimmed with embroidered fleur-de-lis. The cloth-of-gold weavers came in robes of their own cloth of gold, their servants, in purple taffeta. Only the master cotton dealers—probably to advertise their more modest wares—were simply clad. Their cloaks were fustian.

The guildsmen did not rely on cloaks and costumes alone to catch the eyes of the spectators. The master woolworkers, marching two by two, carried olive branches in their hands and wore crowns of olive leaves. Even the humbler master shoemakers wore golden circlets on their brows, and these were crowned with pearls.

Every guild had its banner borne before it, and these were of every possible color. Most of the guilds were proceeded by trumpets and cymbals. Many of them bore gifts. For instance, the master towel- and napkin-makers—and their bookkeepers and apprentices—carried silver flasks filled with wine, and silver cups to serve it in, which they presented to the doge.

Some guilds were proceeded by young boys who sang songs composed for the occasion. But it was the master barbers who put on the most popular show of all. At the head of their contingent were two men mounted on chargers and clad and armed as knights. Behind them they led four captives dressed in foreign garb.

When they reached the doge, one of the two champions dismounted. "Sire," he said respectfully, "we are knights-errant and we have roved the whole world in search of adventure. Now we return with these four prisoners, and we present them to your judgment. If there is any who denies our right to them we are prepared to defend it. Before you and before all of Venice." (Of course, both the knights and the prisoners were master barbers dressed up in costume.)

"There is no one," the doge replied, "and you are welcome here. They are yours by right and by law. I call you quit of all your obligations."

The crowd roared its approval. "Long live the noble doge of Venice!" it roared. "Long live his noble dogaressa!" And the ceremony came to an end.

But you must not think that the great square where all this took place was still the swampy meadow cut by a canal that it was when the Venetians first began to build their city. It had been paved with bricks—not with the stone called trachyte which covers it today—as far back as 1264. In the sixteenth century, when Venice reached its peak, the square and the little piazza next to it were surrounded by almost every one of the handsome buildings that surround it now.

One of the most beautiful of these was the Doge's Palace, and fortunately, we can still see it almost as it was. It was gutted by fire in 1574, and again in 1577, and not only the interior but many great paintings by the Bellini and by Titian and Tintoretto and Veronese were destroyed. Some argued that an entirely new palace should be built, but a committee of five Venetian architects (one of them was Andrea Palladio, the greatest of all Venetian architects) urged the government to rebuild it almost along its old lines, and this was done.

In many ways it is like a cake made of pink and white marble set in diamond-shaped patterns, and iced with gracefully carved battlements and with little towers at each corner. Around the second story is a wide balcony and a colonnade, and around the ground floors an arcade. The capitals of the columns of this arcade are carved with every kind of scene—children engaged in childhood activities, crusaders, famous emperors, virtues and vices, birds, wild animals, trades, nations and peoples, philosophers and lawgivers, and many things more. There is even a carving which shows Noah drinking too much wine.

The interior of the palace is as impressive as the outside. For the most part, it is a succession of spacious rooms, among them the Hall of the College, the Senate Chamber, the Chamber of the Council of Ten, and the Hall of the Great Council. The latter is about a hundred and seventy-five feet long and eighty-seven feet wide. But it had to be large to accommodate all those entitled to sit there.

The whole edifice is built around a courtyard, in the center of which are two bronze wells. They were cast in 1550. On the east side is the Giants' Stairway, so called because of the two huge statues at its head. They represent Mars and Neptune and were done by Jacopo Sansovino.

There is hardly a part of the new building in which some famous artist did not have a hand. For not only were new paintings done to take the place of the old ones, but many of the walls and almost all of the ceilings—including the ceiling over the Scala d'Oro, or Golden Stairway—were studded with gilded designs and lavish paintings. All these were by renowned artists.

The second most beautiful building near St. Mark's Square—some would call it the most beautiful building—

is the Church of St. Mark's. Actually it was the second Church of St. Mark's, for the first, built in 832, was destroyed in 976. The new church was begun in 1063, and consecrated in 1094.

This church is perhaps the most marvelous and the richest of all the Byzantine-style churches which survive. As early as 1071, Doge Selvo ordered every Venetian ship that sailed the seas to bring back anything it could find that would beautify the church, and the Venetians spent their money freely to do this. But after the fall of Constantinople, they did not have to buy. They simply helped themselves to what they wanted, and this included rare marbles and statues from ancient Greek temples; columns and fragments from Roman ruins; icons before which the Byzantines had bowed their heads; and most famous of all, the four huge horses that had once stood in the Byzantine Hippodrome and which the Venetians put above the main door of their church.

These horses became the symbol of Venetian power—so much so that when in 1380 the Genoese admiral stood at the city's threshold, he boasted that he would bit and bridle them. But he did not. That was reserved for Napoleon, who carted them to Paris in 1797. Even so, they were brought back in 1815.

The treasures inside the church are nearly as magnificent as its architecture. Some of them were gifts, some were bought, some appropriated. Here are just a few of them: the sixth-century stone seat of St. Mark's which came from the eastern Mediterranean; a psalter which had once belonged to the Byzantine emperor Basil the Bulgar-slayer; a rock-crystal vase and statuette which had once been on the crown of another Byzantine emperor, Leo VI; a solid-silver reliquary made in the twelfth century; and the Pala d'Oro, or golden altar screen.

"The Pala d'Oro," said a modern art critic, "is the most splendid existing specimen of medieval goldsmiths' and jewelers' work on a large scale that there has ever been." It is also the most precious, for besides eighty-six enamels showing such religious scenes as Christ's entry into Jerusalem, His crucifixion, His descent into hell, His ascension, and the death of the Virgin Mary as well as numerous prophets and saints, it contains two cameos, four topazes, fifteen rubies, seventy balas rubies, ninety amethysts, three hundred emeralds, three hundred sapphires, four hundred garnets, and thirteen hundred and thirty pearls!

But the Doge's Palace with its great rooms and its marvelous paintings, and the church with its lofty domes and priceless treasures were not the only imposing edifices on or near St. Mark's Square. Indeed, it was almost surrounded by magnificent structures.

On the north and south sides were the old and new treasurers' offices (the *Procuratie Vecchie* and the *Procuratie Nuova*), built in 1532 and 1586 respectively. Although they have now turned gray with age, they were once white, and even in the olden days their eaves were the nesting place of the famous swarms of Venetian pigeons.

On the northeast side was the clock where the two Moors —Gog and Magog—struck out the hours, and with such force that one time an English visitor saw the man in charge of them dealt such a blow as he bent over to repair something "that he reeled over the battlements and so broke his neck."

On the southeast corner was the three-hundred-foot *campanile,* from the summit of which could be seen all of

Venice and its lagoon. This was not the *campanile* we see today. The old *campanile* collapsed in 1902 and a new one was completed in 1912. But it is as nearly like the old one as possible.

Finally, on the little piazza which faced the Doge's Palace were the Sansovino Library, the Zecca, or Mint, and the columns of St. Theodore and of the Lion of St. Mark's, between which all criminals were executed. The Zecca, also designed and built by Sansovino, is now the Marciana Library, where Cardinal Bessarion's manuscripts are kept.

St. Mark's Square, however, was not the only part of the city in which Venetians made use of their wealth to pile stone upon stone. There were churches everywhere, and with one exception—Santa Maria della Salute (St. Mary of Good Health), erected between 1630 and 1689 as a thank offering for deliverance from the plague—the best of them were built either before or during Venice's heyday. Far from St. Mark's, too, were the *fondachi* of the foreign merchants. *Fondaco* means warehouse, but actually a *fondaco* was also a consulate and an embassy and a commodity market. Even a few of the public offices were far from the center of the city. For example, the Palazzo dei Camerlenghi—chamberlains, who corresponded to our Internal Revenue Service—was located near the Rialto.

Finally, there were the private palaces which so impressed Francesco Sansovino. They are said to have been two hundred in number, and they were scattered throughout Venice.

"Some of them cost as much as a hundred thousand ducats to build," wrote a visitor from Milan. And yet there were so many of them that you could rent an adequate one for sixty or seventy ducats a year.

The most beautiful of them was the Ca' d'Oro, or House

of Gold, which stood on the Grand Canal in the central part of the city. Like the Doge's Palace, it was pink and white—and in places a very frail blue. Its columns and the four-leafed carvings above them were like lacework made of marble. Architects call it Gothic—but it could also be called Arab, for it was like an enchanted palace from the Arabian Nights. But then, Arab influence was always strong in Venice, and the Venetian noblemen who built it had traded widely in the Near East.

But if the Ca' d'Oro was the most beautiful, it was only one of the many beautiful palaces in Venice. There were others everywhere and in every style of architecture. But though the architecture differed, they were almost always built on the same plan.

First of all there was a courtyard with a well in it, almost always marble, and beautifully carved. The ground-floor rooms around this were usually either storerooms or offices, since the Venetian almost always conducted his business from his home. A marble stairway led from the courtyard to the second story, which housed the living quarters. Here there was a large reception hall, the walls of which were either decorated by some well-known artist or hung with tapestries. Tapestries had the advantage of helping keep the room warm, and this was important in December and January. This hall usually had a fireplace with a handsome marble mantlepiece. Beyond the hall were bedrooms and a kitchen. There was often a library too, and in it were not only books but musical instruments with which to while away long evenings.

There was almost always a garden. The Venetian gardens at Murano and the Giudecca were famous and few Venetians who could afford it were without one.

Incidentally, if you had a garden, you could offer other kinds of entertainment than lute playing or conversation. This was the case with one Girolamo Sinistro, a wealthy Venetian. "As soon as anyone enters your court," a friend wrote him, "you spread before his eyes hen turkeys, Italian peacocks, cranes, geese, ostriches, badgers, and owls as well as rare conies, little foxes, and little hares. Next he mounts the stairs and here he sees rock pipits, goldfinches, and linnets. And that's not all. For in one place a magpie chatters, in another a parrot talks, and elsewhere a monkey plays his tricks. No duke has a more marvelous park."

The plain people and the artisans lived well too. Almost entirely gone were the wooden houses of earlier days, and the citizen—in the class below the noblemen—was beginning to live in comfort and ease. To be sure, he did not have the same expensive furnishings or wear the same expensive clothes as did those whose names were written in the Libro d'Oro. But his house was usually well built and two or three stories high. It almost always had a balcony. And on the roof there was almost always an *altana* of the sort that adorned the house of his nobleman neighbor. His wife's hair did not have to be neglected.

Even a humble gondolier did not do badly. He did not live in a hovel but in a decent house, and although he had no paintings by Titian or Tintoretto, his walls were at least hung with portraits of his forebears by some less famous artist, and these portraits were almost always draped with banners he or they had won in some regatta. His food was good if plain, and it was adequate. He had wine, country wine, to be sure, but it was drinkable and abundant. He had a dark-haired wife—only a few of this class took the trouble to tint their hair—and a dozen or so bright-eyed children.

And if he sang as he rowed his little vessel—later and almost until modern times he would sing verses from Tasso's *Jerusalem Delivered,* one of the great poems of Italian literature—it was because his heart was full.

Four
Ships Sail
to Calicut

Unfortunately the happy state of Venetian affairs did not last forever. Such a state of affairs never does. That is one of the lessons we learn from history. A nation is like a human being. It has its childhood; its youth (that is when it is daring and adventurous); its manhood (when it enjoys what it has won in earlier days); and finally its old age.

Venice was no exception. It was no different from the ancient Egypt of the Pharaohs, which became a province of the conquering Romans; or Babylon with its ziggurats and hanging gardens, which once ruled from the mountains of Iran to the Red Sea, and now is crumbled ruins; or the Roman Empire founded by Julius Caesar, which was toppled by the very barbarians who drove the ancestors of the Venetians to the lagoons; or the Spain of the *conquistadores*; or the British Empire, on which the sun once never set, but which has been slowly but surely declining in our own day.

In part, this was the Venetians' own fault. Life in Venice had come to be so good that they were no longer willing to leave it, especially for the risky and uncomfortable business of foreign trade. Some no longer even manned their own ships. After the sixteenth century, chained slaves took the place of free citizens at the oars of their galleys, and now even the captains were frequently paid hands instead of part owners. They were often foreigners.

In contrast, those Venetians who were still eager for deeds of daring on the salt sea usually found that they did better if they sought employment elsewhere. For example, John Cabot, the discoverer of Nova Scotia and Newfoundland, was a Venetian citizen, but he sailed from Bristol, England, under letters patent issued by the English King Henry VII.

Now many Venetians—even the young ones and certainly the rich ones—began to stay at home. Why should they bob up and down in some storm-tossed craft and live in cramped quarters and eat bad food and be wet and seasick and miserable when they could speculate in foreign exchange wherever money-changers gathered? Why should they risk having their ships "docked in sand"—cast ashore—when they could invest in lands and houses on the mainland? Why should they stake all their ducats upon "an argosy bound to Tripolis, another to the Indies, a third to Mexico, and a fourth for England"—this is what Antonio did in *The Merchant of Venice*—when they could turn their hands to industry? And this, many had already done.

It was easier and more pleasant to go into speculation and industry, but it was also less profitable, although the Venetians did not find this out for a while. And there were other factors too. The Venetians lost the ocean commerce that had made them rich and great because of several other important developments over which they had little or no control.

First of all, they lost it because an English princess married the king of Portugal. The English princess was Philippa of Lancaster. Her grandfather was Edward III, her father

John of Gaunt, and she was a niece of the famous Black
Prince. The king of Portugal was João I (John I). A fearless
warrior, he fought and defeated the king of Castile (who
claimed the Portuguese throne) and thus kept his little
country an independent nation. He was known as John the
Great.

João and Philippa had six sons, and the third of them—
a tall, well-built, sunburned man with beetling brows—has
gone down in history as Henry the Navigator. And he de-
served the name. For although after his youth he never
captained a ship or walked a quarterdeck, he had an inborn
love of the sea that came from his English mother, and he
had his father's resources, vigor, and determination, and he
used all of these to promote exploration and discovery with
such zeal that Portugal soon became the foremost seafaring
nation in the world.

He did this in a very thoughtful and methodical way.
When he was twenty-one years old, he helped his father
capture Ceuta on the African side of the Strait of Gibraltar.
There he saw sacks of gold piled in the ruler's palace.

"Where does this gold come from?" he asked.

"From the Niger valley. From the golden land of Guinea."

"Then why not seek it by sea?"

"It has never been done, Your Highness. The way is not
known. There are dangers."

"Then we will make it known."

This he did. Step by step, he sent his ships cautiously
down the African coast, until, in 1434, one of his captains,
Gil Eannes, rounded Cape Bojador, near the southwest corner of Morocco—not too far from where the Vivaldi
brothers had vanished one hundred and fifty years earlier.
This was a milestone, for during the Middle Ages it was
superstitiously believed that no one could go past this cape.

Even that was not enough for Prince Henry. For almost at this very time, his brother, Prince Pedro, returned from Venice with a handsomely bound manuscript of *The Travels of Marco Polo*, which he gave to Henry. Henry read the book avidly, and then even standing at the door of tropical Africa seemed a small achievement.

"We must go further than this!" he cried. "We must sail around the dark continent itself, and come to all these riches. We must send ambassadors to the court of Prester John in Abyssinia." (Abyssinia is today's Ethiopia, and Prester John was the legendary medieval Christian monarch who was said to rule somewhere in Africa or Asia and to be a lineal descendant of the Queen of Sheba.) "From there we must sail our ships to India and then to the Spice Islands and to Cathay!"

Unfortunately, Henry himself did not live long enough to see this come to pass, but he did take almost all the steps that were necessary to make it possible.

The most important one was the setting up of the Villa do Infante, or City of the Prince, on Sagres (the Sacred Cape), a promontory which jutted out into the Atlantic and was the most southwesterly point in Europe. Henry's brother Pedro now (1438) served as regent for his nephew, Affonso IV, and Henry had persuaded Pedro to deed the cape to him. On it he established what, for all practical purposes, was the first oceanographic institute in history.

To it came Europe's most distinguished mapmakers, ship designers, astronomers, and navigators. Columbus himself visited Sagres before he set out on his voyages.

The Prince's City was a headquarters for every kind of nautical knowledge, and from it, under Henry's orders, sailed captain after well-trained captain—among them Andrea Barbarigo's onetime agent, Cadamosto.

These men discovered Senegal and Sierra Leone in Africa and even reached a point where the coast turned southeast. But that was as far as they went during Henry's lifetime, for each journey could be only a little longer than the last journey, and each journey took a very long time.

Twenty-eight years later, however, it was another matter. In 1486 King João II ordered Bartholomew Diaz to sail down the African coast as far as he could. Diaz reached a point a good one thousand miles further than any other European had ever gone, and was then blown southward by a wild gale. He and his men sped before it for thirteen days, and then, chilly and drenched, they turned east and next north. In due course they came to a sheltered bay on the shores of which Hottentot natives herded their cattle. There Diaz explored the coast for a while, until his crew forced him to turn back toward Portugal. It was only then that he discovered that he had rounded the cloud-crowned cape that marks the southernmost tip of the continent. Remembering his experiences, he named it the Stormy Cape, but João, dreaming of his great-uncle's longing to reach India, rechristened it the Cape of Good Hope.

In 1497 another rough-and-ready Portuguese sea captain made the hope a reality. His name was Vasco da Gama, and on July 8, he set sail from Lisbon with four ships and a hundred and seventy men. Driven by west winds—near the Cape Verde Islands, Vasco had made a wide sweep into the South Atlantic Ocean so as to get their benefit—he soon reached the cape discovered by Diaz, and then sailed up the East African coast to the Arab port of Malindi in present-day Kenya. There native sailors told him that the monsoon (a wind that blows steadily from the southwest all summer long) would carry him over twenty-five hundred miles of scorching ocean to the land he sought. He took one of them on as a pilot—he had to do this if he wanted to avoid the coral shoals of the Laccadive Islands—and after bounding over a blue sea, dropped anchor in Calicut (now Kozhikode), on the marshy, mangrove-bordered Malabar coast of India, on May 20, 1498.

Da Gama and his men gaped at what they saw, for between five and seven hundred vessels—every kind, from their own caravels to Arab dhows and even Chinese junks —swung lazily at their cables in the harbor. And when they stepped ashore, the bazaars were overflowing with everything the Portuguese had ever dreamed of or wanted.

For a while Vasco was received coldly by the dusky *samorin* (local prince) of the place, but he skillfully got into the good graces of other coastal rulers, and before long the holds of his vessels were bulging. Then he turned homeward again, and in August, 1499, with two of his vessels—the other two had been lost or abandoned—and the fifty-five men who still survived, he was in Lisbon again, unloading sack after sack of precious spices. These were so valuable that they not only compensated the dangers and hardships of the two-year voyage but much more than paid for its expenses.

Small wonder the Portuguese were exultant. The spice trade was the most profitable trade carried on by western merchants, and for a long time it had been a Venetian monopoly. Year after year, the ships of Venice sailed to Alexandria—or to Beirut and other cities which the Egyptians ruled—and there loaded their fragrant cargoes. It was the only way spices came to Europe.

But now the Portuguese could get these commodities directly by sea without paying either the exorbitant prices charged by the Egyptian middleman or the heavy duties exacted by the Egyptian sultan. Nor could the Venetians follow in their footsteps. For not only had more than one

pope granted the Portuguese exclusive rights to all naviga-
tion down the African coast, but armed Portuguese vessels
kept a watchful eye upon the Strait of Gibraltar. If a vessel
turned south, it risked being intercepted. Furthermore, the
Portuguese were the only ones who had any real knowledge
of these new roads to the East, and they kept this a closely
guarded secret.

"Your excellencies," a Portuguese official wrote the Venetian government, "have no need to go to Egypt any more for
the spices you want. Indeed, you will not find them there.
Instead, come to Lisbon where we can supply all you need.
You will be treated courteously here, and made to feel at
home."

But the Venetians did not have to be told this by the
Portuguese. At least, the wise ones didn't. They understood
only too well what was now at stake. "We stand at the edge
of a precipice," wrote a merchant, "and our commerce may
be facing its death sentence—this commerce is the very
cornerstone of our wealth and power." It turned out that his
gloomy forebodings were only too true.

In 1502—only three years after Vasco had returned to
Portugal—the Beirut convoy brought back to Venice only
four bales of pepper and the Alexandria convoy only two or
three. This may have been because Portuguese competition
—or the Portuguese blockade—had driven prices too high.
It was worse in 1504. Then the ships came back from Egypt
with holds empty. "This is something," cried a merchant on
the Rialto, wringing his hands, "that has never happened
before!"

Even at that, if the new Portuguese route to India had
been all that the Venetians had to contend with, they might
still have retained their first place among maritime nations,
for they had learned all the tricks of the trade from their

years of experience, and they now devoted all their knowledge and energy to solving the problems they faced.

They immediately sent some of their most skilled diplo-
mats to Portugal, and these made it their business to find out
all they could about this terrible threat. How many ships
sailed to India and how often? How much time did a voyage
take? What were the new routes exactly? Perhaps, despite
Portuguese secrecy, they could find out. What were the haz-
ards, if any? How much did the expeditions cost? What
were the profits? What were the intentions of the king of
Portugal? Was his aim peaceful competition, or war to seize
all the trade with India?

This last question was particularly important, for re-
ports reached the lagoons that Vasco had been ordered to
station vessels at the entrance to the Red Sea and to sink or
capture all Arab or Egyptian craft sailing for the spice ports.

What, finally, would the Indians themselves do?

Here the Venetian ambassadors used every kind of per-
suasion they could think of. More than one Indian emissary
had come to Lisbon either with da Gama or later, and the
Venetian ambassadors sought them out and talked to them.
In a way, they really warned them.

"Portugal is a poor country," they said. "True, she has
sent ships to your shores, but only a few ships. She cannot
send more, for she has no more to send. Only Venice can
provide the great fleets that your commerce really needs,
and she certainly will not put them at the disposal of her
rival. If you are wise, you will continue to deal with Venice."

At the same time, the Republic of Venice applied every
kind of pressure at their disposal to Egypt. To that land,
too, they sent a special embassy. It was in the charge of
Benedetto Sanudo, who knew the Egptian trade well, so well

that he did not really need the secret instructions that he was given. "The situation is very grave," he was told to say to the sultan, "and you must take strong and positive steps."

He suggested two of them: First, the sultan must persuade the Indians to close their ports to the Portuguese. He must convince them that if they did not do this, they would risk the whole Arab-Egyptian trade. And second, he must lower the prices that the Egyptians were charging the Venetians for the spices which they bought in Egypt. Only if this were done could the Venetians meet the new competition that was taking trade—and profits—from Egypt quite as much as from Venice.

But the Egyptians obviously couldn't do the first, and they wouldn't do the second.

How could they persuade the Indians to close their ports when Vasco da Gama's fleet of four was followed by eight vessels commanded by Pedro Alvarez Cabral—who detoured westward and discovered Brazil before rounding the Cape of Good Hope—and by the even larger fleet commanded by Albuquerque? How could they when the Portuguese were even beginning an empire of their own with trading posts at Cochin and Goa?

How could the Egyptians tell the Indians not to trade with Lisbon when other heavily-armed Portuguese vessels—to the Venetians they were pirates, but they flew the flag of Portugal and sailed under the order of King Manuel the Fortunate—were now roving the Red Sea, burning and sinking every Egypt-bound vessel they encountered and seizing its cargo? When they were cruising off Mozambique and Madagascar looking for Arab craft blown there by the summer monsoon? When they had even built a fort on the mountainous island of Socotra—one of the hottest and most humid places in the world—which commanded the approaches to the Gulf of Aden through which all ships must pass?

As to lowering spice prices, Egyptian revenues were shrinking rapidly enough without further reducing them. Let the Venetians do the price reducing.

No was the answer, and Ambassador Sanudo could do nothing but return gloomily to Venice and report this to the government. He did.

But no was not an answer that the Venetians would—or could—take. Out went a second ambassador, and this time he did not beg. He threatened.

"We now have no choice," he said, "but must do business with the Portuguese. Their products are now flooding every market in Europe—not only London and the Low Countries but even the German markets in Augsburg and Nuremberg. But they would still like our ships to carry these goods, and many of our merchants are already insisting that we do. In that way, we would make at least *some* of the profits."

"And in doing this, bow your heads to these newcomers and interlopers? Be their humble servants?" said the sultan.

"Then at least join with us in digging a canal through Suez," replied the ambassador. "Then we can sail directly to India as the men from Lisbon do." (This was in 1506, four hundred and sixty-five years before a canal was actually completed. However, the idea was an old one. The Egyptians had thought of it in 1300 B.C.)

But this did not please the sultan any more than the suggestion that he lower his prices. To be sure, Egypt could have collected tolls, but it would have ended forever her profitable role as a buyer, then seller. So he merely smiled. "It is your trade, not our trade, that the Portuguese have taken. It is up to you, not us, to do something." And the Venetians had done little enough, he said. Particularly for the prosperity of Egypt!

"Once upon a time," the sultan continued, "you used to send seven galleys to Alexandria and five to Beirut, and they were all laden with merchandise. Now you hardly send one of them. Once upon a time, your goods stored in our warehouses were worth three hundred thousand ducats. Now they are scarcely worth eighty thousand ducats! Do you deal only in spices? We have other things to sell you." He named oil and copper, and probably he could have named wheat. "Again, it is not up to me but to you to do something!"

But the Venetians could not, try as they did—and they did try, even appointing a five-member special spice committee and giving it full power to act—for a new enemy had by now appeared on the scene and dealt the final blow.

This enemy was the Ottoman Turk, a hard-riding nomad people from Central Asia who, around 1280, arrived in the mountainous part of Anatolia (present-day Asiatic Turkey) and before many years had extended their rule to the Sea of Marmara and then to large areas in the Balkan Peninsula. When the Turks reached the salt water, they took to the waves and shortly became such skilled seamen that they did not fear to challenge the bridegroom of the sea itself for mastery of the eastern and then the western Mediterranean.

In the beginning, Venice and the Turks were on reasonably amicable terms. "We are merchants and we have to learn to live with everybody," said a Venetian when his city was criticized for signing a trade agreement with this infidel nation in 1384.

As an example, the Venetians refused to take part in a crusade organized against the Turk by the Byzantine emperor, Manuel II. They were irked because his new line of Byzantine emperors, who had driven out the pro-Venetian Latin line set up in 1204, were systematically trying to pare down Venetian powers. But the Venetians refused, even though Manuel promised, in return for their help, to make amends by giving them complete control of Constantinople as well as the important islands of Imbros and Lemnos, which dominated the approaches to the Dardanelles. And when the Turkish sultan Bajazet (1389–1403) was taken prisoner by Tamerlane the Great (who paraded him through Asia in an iron cage), the Venetians did nothing more than seize or purchase an outpost here or there, and these were mainly islands or cities owned by the Greeks.

But in 1453 Mohammed II—the first Turk really trained to be an emperor—surrounded the Byzantine capital with a fleet of four hundred and ninety-three vessels and an army of two hundred thousand men, and beat down its thousand-year-old walls with his enormous cannon. With that the Byzantine Empire fell, and it was another story.

War to the death between Venice and the Turks became inevitable. They both thought of themselves as the heir to the fallen empire. They both wanted to control the areas which it had ruled.

This war broke out almost immediately, and during its first sixty years, it was a never-ending seesaw. The Turks would win a series of battles. Towns and islands would be taken, the Venetian bailiff and his noblemen either sawed in half or impaled, and the other inhabitants sold into slavery. Next the Venetians would win a few fights and a large part of what they had lost would be restored to them. It went this way year after year.

But in the long run, the Turks won more often than they were defeated, and at one time Turkish armies even crossed the Isonzo and the Tagliamento rivers in Italy itself. The smoke of burning villages could be seen from Venice. Finally, except for Cyprus, which the Venetians had recently won, and Crete, about all that was left of the Venetian empire was Patras and a few other towns on the Greek mainland and a few Aegean islands.

And now a last disaster came. Since it was no longer necessary for the Turks to devote all their attention to the city of the lagoons, they were free to deal with other problems. And what they did affected Venice. A new sultan, Selim the Saint, sat on the Turkish throne and it irked him to see an independent ruler in Egypt. He must be the master of the Moslem world with no competitor, and this he could not be if there was another sultan in Cairo. Especially he must be master of the Moslem world in Africa. That is—and this was his intention—if he was to make the Mediterranean a Turkish lake.

He set out to make himself master with every force at his disposal. Selim became sultan in 1512, when he was forty-six years old, and by 1514, he had moved into northern Iran and had conquered Azerbaidzhan, Kurdistan, and part of Iraq. (This removed pressure from his left flank.) He spent the winter in Tabriz under the twelve-thousand-foot-high Mt. Sahand. Then in 1515 he marched on Syria, where in the next two years he defeated the Egyptians in a series of decisive battles. The road to Egypt was now open to him. In 1517, Egypt fell in his hands.

This was a death knell to the last Venetian hope.

The naval battles with the Turk had already damaged these hopes greatly, for Venice had been obliged to commit most of her ships to fighting them. The Egyptians knew this, and so when the doge had threatened to transfer Venice's trade to Lisbon, they knew that he was bluffing. They knew that Venice had hardly enough ships left for her old trade routes and could not take on any new ones.

But when Selim had conquered Egypt, Venice could not even threaten, for a new and very different people now held the gateway to the East.

Make no mistake about it: the Mamelukes—the sultans who ruled Egypt before the Turks overthrew them—always drove a hard bargain. They understood trade just as well as the Venetians did, and had no scruples whatever about taking advantage of their geographical position. They had no scruples about using any means they could to accumulate the wealth they needed to make their country one of the richest—and most brilliant—in the sixteenth-century world. But until just at the end, when they seem to have miscalculated the havoc that the Portuguese voyages would wreak, they never carried their acquisitiveness too far. Although they extracted all the profit they could, they did not kill the goose that laid the golden egg.

But the Turks were still at heart the same people as their nomad ancestors. They took. They did not produce. Trade, then, meant very little to them (at any rate, they did not understand trade), and they hated the Venetians. What better way to show this hatred than to destroy something they did not want, and that the Venetians needed and loved?

Systematically, they set out to destroy the trade with the Far East. To name just one thing, they rounded up all the spice merchants in Cairo, Alexandria, and Beirut and forced them to set up their places of business in Istanbul (Constantinople's new name). But there was no spice business in this city or anywhere else where the Turks ruled!

As a result, the Near-East trade with India and the Far East, which had flourished since the days of the Caesars if not longer, simply vanished. The markets were not merely empty but deserted. Although the Turks allowed the Venetians to maintain a consulate in Alexandria, its head was only a vice-consul, not a consul. And so few were the Venetians who still remained there that he was often hard put to find twelve of them to sit on his council as required by Venetian law.

It was not only, then, because the Venetians had grown soft and comfort-loving, and because the Portuguese had found a new and better way to the Orient that Venice lost her rule of the sea, and lost too the riches it brought her. It was this love of comfort *and* the new sea routes *and* one thing more: the Turks and their newly acquired naval abilities. It was these three things together that finally started Venice on her way to becoming just another city.

Venice Later and Today

Despite these crushing blows, Venice remained an independent state, and for nearly three hundred years more, it remained an important one. Somehow, it also managed to remain a wealthy state—at least for a while.

John Evelyn, an English royalist who fled his country so as not to swear allegiance to Cromwell's Roundhead parliament, visited Venice in 1646. He found it just as dazzling as it had ever been.

The marriage with the sea was still celebrated with its old pomp. As always, the doge, clad in Byzantine robes, was followed by a swarm of galleys and gondolas, the latter with highly-polished steel beaks. The Rialto was thronged with merchants and would have seemed active to one who had not seen it a century before. The only difference was that the merchants now crossed to it over the new bridge which had been built in 1591 to replace the old wooden one.

"It was of one arch," said John Evelyn, "and this arch was large enough for a galley to pass under it." (The old bridge had had three arches with a drawbridge in the center.) "It

was built of good marble, and had on it, besides many
pretty shops, three ample and stately passages. The two
outermost were nobly balustered with the same stone."

He could still call the Merceria "one of the most delicious
streets in the world," and note that it was tapestried on both
sides, and for its whole length, with cloth of gold, rich damasks, and expensive silks, which were hung from the balconies of the houses and shops.

Even the arsenal seemed to be flourishing. It buzzed and
hummed almost as much as it had when Venice was ship-
master to most of Europe and had to maintain large fleets.
Like all other visitors to Venice, Evelyn was taken to see it,
and like most of them, he was willing to say that it seemed
to him "one of the best furnished in the world."

He entered it through a strongly guarded gate, and after
mounting a stairway, came into a gallery with enough arms
for a thousand men, followed by a second gallery for saddles.
This was decorated with standards taken from the enemy.

Then came row after row of forges—thirteen in a single
shed—where smiths were beating anchors into shape; a car-
penter shop, where oars and masts for a hundred vessels were
being made; and a foundry, where the Venetians cast their
huge cannons, one of which weighed 16,573 pounds!

Nearby was storage for the ordnance of twelve galleasses
—warships one hundred and fifty feet long with a comple-
ment of thirteen hundred men—and beyond this, slips for
fifty galleys and room to build as many more.

There was also a rope walk two hundred yards long; a
warehouse for hemp; a saltpeter house; and sheds to protect
the ships from bad weather. Finally, there was a room full
of guns of all sizes, some of which discharged "six times at
once," a courtyard full of "cannons, bullets, chains, grap-
ples, grenadoes, etc.," and another room which contained

arms for eighty thousand men as well as weapons of offense and defense for sixty-two ships, and thirty-two pieces of artillery taken from the Turks.

Five hundred workmen were still employed, and if that was a lot less than in the days of old, it was still a goodly number.

"They march in and out in military order every evening and receive their pay through a small hole in the gate where the governor lives," Evelyn wrote.

He also noted that although the principal Venetian fleets were at sea, there were at least twenty-three galleys still docked there. "Twenty-three galleys and four great galleys!" The latter were like nothing seen in England, which was only beginning to be a great sea power.

"They have one hundred oars on each side!" Evelyn exclaimed. That meant two hundred oarsmen on each vessel, to say nothing of the rest of the crew.

A century after Evelyn's visit the city still gleamed—or at least it appeared to.

A French statesman, De Brosses, found it unique when he visited it in 1739. "It is like no other city in the character of its people, in its way of living, in the freedom that reigns there, and in the peace and tranquility which all enjoy."

St. Mark's Square was still the most wonderful piazza in the world. Not even De Brosses' own dearly-loved Place Vendôme in Paris surpassed it. Its women—but especially the women of the people—were the most beautiful.

Another Frenchman praised it for its government, and said that even in these degenerate days, it was the school to which wise rulers went to learn their lessons.

But it was not only Frenchmen who thought that Venice was the wonder of the world. The Holy Roman emperor Joseph II of Austria; King Gustavus III of Sweden; and finally, "the Count of the North," who was really Czar Paul I of Russia—all visited Venice during the eighteenth century and were dazzled by receptions that would have bankrupted their own treasuries.

The great German poet Goethe spent a few months there in 1787, and he too found it "a marvelous monument." It was "rich and extraordinary," he said, "and it came forth from the bosom of the sea just as the goddess Athena came forth from the temple of Zeus."

Palaces—some of them very fine indeed—were still being built, and churches too, and important public works still engaged the attention of the Great Council. It was in these late days that the Murazzi, a four-mile-long sea wall, was built to protect the lagoons, and that the main channel leading to the city was widened and deepened. By doing this, Venice hoped to retain such of its once far-flung foreign commerce as still remained. The republic also tried to entice new commerce by sending agents abroad. Among other things, these agents tried to persuade Trieste and Ancona to become free ports—although it is hard to see why, since Venice now had so little commerce that she could hardly have used them.

In the world of culture, Venice still flourished too.

The only great writer Venice ever produced lived in the days of her decline. This was Carlo Goldoni, who wrote more than two hundred and sixty plays, most of them comedies. The Venetians loved them, for they portrayed the everyday life in Venice, and if they poked fun at it, they did so in a very good-natured way.

There were two other Venetian comedy writers in those days—Pietro Chiari and Carlo Gozzi—and all three always played to packed houses. To rowdy and tumultuous packed houses, for each of the three had his own noisy supporters,

and when a play by one of them was put on, the supporters
of the other two filled the house with loud guffaws, shouted
conversation, fits of coughing, ostentatious yawning, cock-
adoodledoos, and catcalls. Then, when the curtain went
down, they adjourned to the Café of the Cat on a Leash to
argue until dawn.

Music also flourished. There were four conservatories in
Venice, and one famous musician after another came and
stayed there. Among them were Claudio Monteverdi, who
was one of the first men to compose operas, and Baldassare
Galuppi, about whom Robert Browning wrote one of his
best-known poems.

In these later days, the Venetians loved music so much
that they even dated happenings after an opera singer. After
Senhora Todi, a Portuguese singer, had appeared in Venice,
the Venetians dated their letters: "Venice, in the year of La
Todi." Once they had dated them in the year of one of their
great victories.

Not even Venetian painting had lost all its wonder. Titian,
Tintoretto, and Veronese had long since disappeared, but a
number of new painters took their place, and if they were
not as great as their predecessors, their pictures were highly
regarded throughout the world. You will almost certainly
have heard of four of them: Giovanni Battista Tiepolo, who
did religious and mythological scenes; Rosalba Carriera,
who painted delicate portraits; and Antonio Canaletto and
Francesco Guardi, whose paintings show Venice with its
squares and canals and people in these sunset days.

Finally, it was during these days of Venice's decline that
one of the greatest of all Venetian patriots lived and died.

Paolo Sarpi, born in 1552, was a Servite monk, and there
is no question that he was a loyal son of the Church. But he
was loyal to his native Venice too, and when Pope Paul V

placed the city under interdict for refusing to release two priests her government had imprisoned for scheming against her, he came to her aid.

"Render unto Caesar the things that are Caesar's" was the Venetian argument. But they reversed its emphasis. "Support the pope in religious matters," they said, "but your government in political ones."

Sarpi said Venice was right. He was trained in theology, and he came out of his convent to write pamphlet after pamphlet attacking the Vatican and saying that the pope had no right to give Venice orders in a matter that concerned her security.

In return, he was attacked by Paul, who summoned him to Rome to stand trial for heresy. He refused to go. Then an attempt was made to murder him. Armed ruffians attacked him as he was leaving the Doge's Palace and left him for dead, but he recovered from his serious wounds. Undiscouraged, he finally worked out a compromise which both sides could accept. Venice surrendered the priests to King Henry IV of France and he, not Venice, released them. Thus Venice kept her independence and yet the pope was satisfied.

From then on, Sarpi was a hero to every Venetian, and he loved Venice as much as Venice loved him. Even his last words were a prayer for her. As he lay dying, he said: "*Esto perpetua*—may you live forever!"

But even if Venice seemed to some, if not to all, to be as glorious as she ever was, those who had clear eyes could see that she was on the decline.

For one thing, the never-ending war with the Turks went on. The latter, far from being content with their conquest of Egypt, set out systematically to drive the Venetians out of the eastern Mediterranean. It was a slow process but a steady one. In 1522, the Turks captured Rhodes, just off the

Turkish coast. Their excuse was that it was a hotbed of
Catalan and Maltese pirates, and it probably was. They
forced its defenders, the Knights of Rhodes—a military
order founded during the First Crusade—to take refuge in
Malta. This the Knights held, still fighting Turkish corsairs,
until the time of Napoleon. In 1537, the great Turkish admiral Khair-ed-Din besieged Corfu, off the coast of Greece,
and for a while shut Venice up in the Adriatic. Finally, in
1570, the Turks took Cyprus—this is the war Shakespeare
writes about in *Othello*—but here their cruelty almost undid
them.

The capital, Nicosia, fell almost without a shot being fired,
but Famagusta, seaport and Venetian stronghold, held out
for eleven months, although Turkish cannon—and Turkish
artillery was as fine as any in the world—battered it both
night and day, and every avenue of escape or rescue had
been cut off by Turkish fleets.

But at last treachery did what force could not do.

"I will spare everybody in the city if you yield to me,"
the Turkish admiral, Mustafa, said to the Venetian general,
Marcantonio Bragadino. Since his people had by now been
reduced to eating cats and even rats, Bragadino surrendered.

But no sooner had he done this than Mustafa broke every
promise he had made. "You have slain fifty thousand
Turks," he cried, "and you must pay for this!"

In particular, Mustafa turned his wrath on Bragadino. He
had him killed with horrible tortures and later sent his
stuffed skin to the sultan as a trophy. But Bragadino was
not his only victim. Almost to a man, he had the valiant defenders impaled and the women and children sold into slavery.

When the tidings of this reached Europe, a shock wave of
horror ran from land to land, and some of the powers even

forgot their quarrels long enough to organize a holy league. Pope Pius V, Philip of Spain, and the Venetians were the leaders, and when a fleet of two hundred vessels was assembled, even little Monaco contributed one or two. The commander was Don John of Austria, Philip's half brother, and the most dashing soldier of the age.

Don John sailed straight for Greece, where he knew that the Turks would be waiting for him. At Lepanto, near the Gulf of Patras, he met their fleet. It numbered three hundred vessels, all drawn up in the shape of the Turkish crescent.

"Attack them at once!" ordered John, although he saw that he was outnumbered. But if he was brave he was not foolhardy, and he first saw to it that four huge galleasses equipped with heavy guns were towed into position in front of his fleet. The weight of the shot they fired broke up repeated countercharges, and the Turks were routed. Only thirty of their vessels were able to escape. They lost twenty-five thousand sailors.

This took place on October 7, 1571, and a few days later a Venetian warship, *Gabriel the Archangel*, came racing in past the Lido. Flags and pennons flew from her spars and she was laden with every kind of trophy.

"Victory!" her crew shouted. "Victory over the Turk! Victory! Victory!"

At once every bell in the city began to toll, and a thick pall of smoke hung over the arsenal as the cannon thundered in salute. At the sound, the Venetians poured out of their houses until the streets and the piazzas were overflowing. A procession started in which captured standards were trailed in the dirt, and captured Turkish turbans were paraded on the tips of pikes and lances. But in contrast to Famagusta, not a single Turkish resident was either killed or molested, and the Fondaco de' Turchi was not even damaged.

Then and only then, the rejoicing citizens filed reverently into their great church, and there, in the presence of the doge, who was clad in his magnificent robes, they solemnly sang a grateful *Te Deum.*

But the victory was only a temporary one.

Even though the Turkish sultan, another Selim, Selim the Drinker, was one of the weakest they had ever had, the Turks put together another fleet within a year, and it roved the seas again. In the meantime, Don John—and Pope Pius, King Philip of Spain, and the other Venetian allies—had lost most of their enthusiasm.

"We have done what we set out to do," they said. "Why should we fight any longer? The Turks are now afraid to attack us, and so why should we care about the lost Venetian empire? Let the Venetians win it back themselves—that is, if they want it and are able to."

Obviously, the Venetians wanted to—but it was quite clear too that they could not. That is, if no one would help them. For although victorious, they had not defeated the Turks without paying a heavy price. In the battle of Lepanto alone, Venice had lost five thousand men and a goodly share of her ships. Besides that, she had suffered heavy losses at Cyprus and in other places. Moreover, the treasury was almost empty.

So, hat in hand, the proud conquerors of a great Turkish fleet went to the very men they had beaten, to sue for an ignominious peace.

On March 7, 1573, it was granted to them. Under the terms of the treaty signed that day, Venice agreed to pay war indemnities of three hundred thousand ducats—indemnities for having dared to defend what was her own. She also agreed to double the tribute she was already paying for the right to hold the island of Zante, which had been hers for years. Venice had no choice here. She had to hold Zante if she was even to pretend to protect her own shores, not merely from the Turks but from corsairs and pirates, who were as plentiful there in those days as they were later near the Spanish Main.

Venice also agreed to give back all her recent conquests in Dalmatia. She had made quite a few while the Turks were trying to fight off the Holy League. Finally, she agreed to accept, and accept formally, the fact that her overseas empire had virtually vanished—that it had been reduced to Crete (but at least Crete was a good base for future operations), and those Dalmatian and Ionian islands which had been hers for seven centuries, and a few small seaports in the Aegean.

"You might almost think that the Turks had won the battle!" said a Venetian sadly. You almost might!

Moreover, this was to happen over and over again. Venice won many a battle, and sometimes she even won a war, only to lose all at the peace table—or to lose all even before she got there—because although she stood guard for all Europe against the Turks, nobody came to her side.

In the end, she could take no more, and in 1718 Venice gave up almost all of the little she still held: Crete, which she had lost after a heroic defense but then won again; the Morea, which had been conquered in 1688 by the last great Venetian leader, Francesco Morosini; Tinos in the Greek islands; and Antivari (Bar) and Dulcigno (Ulcinj) in Albania. Indeed, except for a few small places in the latter country, all Venice was allowed to retain was the city itself and her territories on the Italian mainland.

Soon even the mainland seemed hardly worth fighting for.

"So sweet and longed for to us is peace," it was said in

the city, "that we turn away our eyes from any danger that threatens us. We only hope that it will not come too near." This point of view is easy to understand.

For besides her losses in ships and equipment and men —and these were very great—Venice had spent a hundred and twenty-six million ducats in the last twenty-five year period of her wars with Turkey, and this had got her nothing. Why should she spend more?

But it was not merely this long series of expensive wars that had hurried Venice toward her last days. The Venetians themselves had changed—and not for the better.

When Venice first began to lose her profitable foreign trade—or found that it was too difficult and risky to sustain —she turned her hand to industry. But now not even industry appealed to the Venetians, for they were interested not in making money but in squandering it.

Squander it they did!

The men squandered it on French tailors and on powdered wigs—some of these cost as much as a thousand dollars apiece; on embroidered vests, ruffled shirts, and silken knee breeches; on gold-headed canes and liveried serving men— and on their barbers.

The women spent extravagantly too. The hairdresser— the eighteenth-century equivalent of a modern beauty parlor —took the place of the confessional. It cost a fortune to go there, but those who did heard all the latest gossip, or perhaps even arranged for a meeting with some handsome young Venetian of whom their parents did not approve.

Nor were the women's costumes—any more than the men's—simple and plain as they had been in the olden days —or at least as they were supposed to have been in the olden days. The inventory of a single wardrobe lists two hundred and thirty separate items, ranging from damasks and brocades imported from Milan and Paris to gold bracelets and enameled buttons. The total value was thirteen hundred and ninety ducats!

Thus garbed, and with a beauty patch strategically placed to show whether the wearer wished to be thought of as saucy and impudent, or passionately in love, or merely flirtatious, and with a fan to enhance their charms, the Venetian beauties went everywhere. They did not stay in their homes as their grandmothers had done.

The Venetians also squandered money on entertainment —on carnivals, plays, and the opera.

Perhaps almost most of all they squandered it on gambling.

The Venetians were not the only gamblers in the world— playing for high stakes was a widespread eighteenth-century vice—but few people spent more time with zechins or even ducats laid out in front of them on tables covered with green baize. These they staked on the turn of a card or a throw of dice as they played faro, basset, *biribisso* (a sort of backgammon), and other games of chance. Of course, there were some winners, such as the beautiful lady who, we are told, broke the bank in four or five plays. She could live for a year on what the croupier pushed toward her. But few were that fortunate. For example, one nobleman lost seventeen thousand ducats in a single evening.

Worst of all, the Venetians could no longer afford any of this. They could not afford to support fleets and armies to defend not only themselves but all of Europe. They could not afford their Carnival, even though it brought them thousands of visitors and their money, nor could they afford any of their other lavish extravagances. Least of all could they afford their passion for gambling, although the Venetian government thought they could, and itself long maintained a fashionable and lavish gambling house, the Ridotto, thinking it would reap some of the profits.

The Venetians could only pretend that they could afford these things, and they did this by borrowing heavily and plunging recklessly into debt. But owing money did not trouble them. Indeed, there is a story of a Venetian nobleman who mortgaged his palace on the Grand Canal and his country villa, and sold what was left of his business to give a single dinner party. All of his guests enjoyed it. They did not know that he had rented the china and silverware with borrowed money, that the servants were not his own but hired for the occasion, and that the gold and brocade liveries they wore were rented too.

Nor were the plain citizens and the workingmen any better off. As trade dwindled, unemployment, virtually unknown in the days of old, grew by leaps and bounds. For example, even as early as 1610, only one out of every four shipwrights was employed, yet to Venice the shipbuilding industry was almost as important as the automobile industry is to us. And as the eighteenth century moved to its close, the important glass industry was almost dead, and the wool weavers who had once rivaled the wool weavers of Florence were weaving only six hundred bolts of cloth a year. In the sixteenth century they wove twenty thousand bolts a year!

But nobody seemed to care, and least of all the ruling aristocracy, which was now divided into two factions—the old aristocracy, which was usually poor, and the new aristocracy, which had bought its way into the Libro d'Oro (for sixty thousand ducats paid into the treasury, one could be made an aristocrat) at the time of the Turkish wars. In the old days, the aristocracy had thought of the good of the whole city, but now they were too busy quarreling among themselves. They were too busy trying to keep what they could in their own pockets.

The plain people did not care either. As long as they had their street singers, their circuses, their trained horses and trained dogs, their sellers of quack medicines, cheap perfume, and shoddy trinkets, the times could not be wholly bad. As long as they had their own festivals in their own squares, and their own excursions in flower-decked gondolas to Murano or Mestre, all must be well.

But all was not well—not for Venice anyway—for the winds of change were beginning to blow all over the world, and very soon they would blow Venice down.

They began to blow in France, where, at the very time Venetian noblemen were saying "Let them have carnivals," a French queen was saying "Let them eat cake!"

But there was no cake, or very little, and in 1789, the French Revolution broke out. (By a strange coincidence, Ludovico Manin, who would be the last doge, was elected in that very year.) Down went the terrible prison of the Bastille; King Louis XVI and his lightheaded queen were forced to abdicate and later guillotined; and the cries of "Liberty, Equality, and Fraternity!" and "Down with the Aristocrats!" were heard in every land.

They were heard even in Venice. In the Great Council itself a few men argued that Venice too must have a democratic government. But no one listened to them. They did not have to. The French were too far away.

Then suddenly the soldier of the Revolution appeared. In 1796 Napoleon Buonaparte marched into Italy and won victory after victory in quick succession. Within weeks, the Kingdom of Sardinia and Piedmont, the Papal States, the duchies of Modena and Parma, and even Naples, one after another, had to sue for peace. It was given to them, but they had to pay for it with cash and with their art treasures.

Venice sued for peace too, but Napoleon turned on her ambassadors scornfully. "The ailing lion of St. Mark need not expect mercy from the conquering general!" he cried. "I will be an Attila to Venice. I do not want any more of your inquisition and your senate. Your government is old and decrepit. It must be destroyed."

He soon found an excuse for doing this. In Verona, which was under Venetian rule, the populace arose one day and massacred every Frenchman the people could find; shortly afterward a French warship was fired upon as it tried to sail in past Fort St. Nicholas on the Lido.

Napoleon's answer was an ultimatum. "Either dissolve your government, or I will declare war on you!"

He barely waited for the Venetians to answer, and when they suggested paying reparations instead, he thundered at them. "Not even the gold of Peru would be enough! Not even if you covered all your beaches with all your ducats!"

On May 1, 1797, he declared war, and within days, he and his armies were on the shores of the lagoon.

On May 12, the Great Council was convened. There were five hundred and thirty-seven members present. Of these, five hundred and twelve voted to accept the French terms. Five abstained from voting. Only twenty proud—and courageous—Venetians dared to vote no.

When the results had been tallied, the doge walked slowly back to his apartment. There he took off his ducal bonnet— the horned hat that was the symbol of his power and authority—and handed it to his valet. "Take it," he said. "Take it as a present. Take it and keep it. I will not need it any more."

Nor would any other doge, for on that day, after eleven

hundred years of glorious existence, the Republic of Venice had come to an end.

It never really came to life again. In October of that same year, Napoleon ceded it to Austria in exchange for Austrian rights in Lombardy. It remained Austrian until 1848.

Then in 1848, another Manin—Daniele Manin, a lawyer —led a successful revolt, and once again there was another Venetian republic. But only for a short while. The Austrians in their white uniforms returned in 1849.

They stayed in Venice until 1866. But in that year, when Italy itself had at last become an independent nation, and when the fires of patriotism were blazing through the land, King Victor Emmanuel, with the assistance of Napoleon III, declared war on the Hapsburg Empire, and in a war that lasted only seven weeks, crushed and defeated it.

Venice was now free again.

But this time—and by a vote of 674,426 to 69!—the city and the Veneto (the Venetian provinces on the mainland) voted to join Italy. Ever since then, Venice has been Italian, and probably she always will be.

Yet even today, Venice does not forget what she once was. To be sure, she has a present as well as a past. Once again she is an important seaport. She has modern docks with modern equipment for loading and unloading, and once again the glass furnaces at Murano turn out their exquisite handiwork. Ships are built in Venice once more, and there are oil, fertilizer, and aluminum industries there. Beautiful lace is still made at Burano. But even so Venice is only the shadow of what she was in the days of her glory, and it is the memory of what she was then that haunts Venetians.

Let us say you go there as a tourist—and I hope you do. You will, of course, ride in a gondola, dodging the little *vaporetti* (steamboats) that take the place of buses and trolleys, and the flashing mahogany speedboats that some think are shaking down the palaces. And as you weave in and out of narrow canals while your gondolier cries stridently: *"Aeol! Sia stali! Sia premi!* Look out! Keep to starboard! Keep to port!" he will not tell you how many ships are built, how much oil is stored, how much glass is shipped, or even how many tourists come—tourists like yourself.

Instead, he will take you back to the past.

"This is the house in which the *poeta* Petrarch lived. Venice gave it to him. Outside of it a ship whose masts were taller than the building was always moored.

"This is Santa Maria de' Frari. The great Tiziano (Titian) is buried here. His home and his garden were in another part of the city.

"Here Enrico Dandolo was born, who conquered Constantinople.

"This palace was built by Badoer (or Corner or Mocenigo or Sanudo) of marble from Istria. It was brought here when Venice was *magnifico*.

"This is the Riva degli Schiavoni—the Quay of the Slavs. On it more merchandise was unloaded in a single day than in most places in a whole year.

"Here—" And he will continue as long as you will listen. Everything that he will have told you is true. But he will have told it to you not because it is true, but because he is proud of Venice, and of its past and history. He is proud of being a Venetian.

I will tell you a story that illustrates this. In Venice, when a gondolier is too old to ply his trade, he becomes what is called a *ganzer,* and stands at one or another of the various landing places with a boat hook in his hands, and lives by the tips which are given him for easing the gondolas in and out.

When I first went to Venice many years ago, I got to know a *ganzer* very well. His name was Antonio Mora; he was eighty-four years old and had a long, heavy white moustache; and he stood straight as the soldier he had probably once been. I used to talk to him as often as I could, and one day I asked him if he could remember when the Austrians were in Venice.

"*Si! Si! Signor!* Yes, indeed, Sir!"

"How did you get rid of them?"

"Boom, boom! Boom, boom, boom! Bang, bang! Cannons. *Fucili!* Boing, boing, boing! Many *fucili!* You say rifles."

"And what happened then?"

"Then the Italians came."

"Then the Italians came? But aren't you an Italian?"

He drew himself up almost as if he were an old Venetian doge.

"Me an Italian?" he said. "Me an Italian? *No! No! Signor!* I am not an Italian. *Sono Veneziano!* I am a Venetian."

I am a Venetian.

I am a true son of that wonderful city and republic which was once so great and glorious, and in its own way gave so much to the world.

Suggestions
for Further Reading

Burckhardt, Jacob, *The Civilization of the Renaissance in Italy*. New York: Harper Torchbooks, 1958.

Crow, John A., *Italy: A Journey Through Time*. New York: Harper & Row, Publishers, 1965.

Hazlitt, W. Carew, *History of the Venetian Republic*, especially Vol. II. New York: AMS Press, 1915.

Lane, Frederic C., *Andrea Barbarigo: Merchant of Venice 1418–1449*. New York: Octagon Books, 1967.

————, *Venetian Ships and Shipbuilders of the Renaissance*. Baltimore: Johns Hopkins Press, 1934.

Laven, Peter, *Renaissance Italy 1464–1534*. New York: G. P. Putnam's Sons, 1966.

Morris, James, *World of Venice*. New York: Vintage Books.

Muraro, Michelangelo, and Grabar, Andre, *Treasures of Venice*. New York: Editions d'Art Albert Skira, 1963.

Okey, Thomas, *The Story of Venice*. New York: E. P. Dutton & Co., 1905.

Pignatti, Terisio, *The Doge's Palace*. New York: Reynal and Company.

Rugoff, Milton, *Marco Polo's Adventures in China*. New York: American Heritage Publishing Co., 1964.

Trease, Geoffrey, *The Italian Story: From the Etruscans to Modern Times*. New York: Vanguard Press, 1963.

Weinstein, Donald, *Ambassador from Venice: Pietro Pasqualigo in Lisbon, 1501*. Minneapolis: University of Minneapolis Press, 1960.

Whelpton, Eric, *A Concise History of Italy*. London: Robert Hale Ltd., 1964.

Index

(The numbers in italics refer to maps.)